beauty care
FOR THE tongue

REVISED
AND UPDATED

LeRoy
Koopman

kregel
PUBLICATIONS

Grand Rapids, MI 49501

Contents

Leader's Guide

The Importance of a Beautiful Tongue

H ow beautiful is your tongue?

Or haven't you considered your tongue in terms of its attractiveness?

You don't often look at it in the mirror.

You don't go shopping for it.

You don't make appointments for it at the tongue beautician.

You don't shop at the cosmetics counter for it.

You don't go to the fitness center for it.

You don't diet to get it in shape.

People don't ogle it, whistle at it, write poems about it, or even smile at it.

It doesn't appear in the centerfold of *Playboy* or *Cosmopolitan.*

Yet it is the tongue—more than the form of your face, or the dimensions of your figure, or the strength of your physique, or the lavishness of your wardrobe, or the size of your income, or the importance of your position in the company—that determines whether or not you are a beautiful person.

>The tongue can give new delights year after year.
>The tongue can turn a plain person into an attractive person.
>The tongue can heal bruises and scrapes.
>The tongue can soothe the agitated temper.
>The tongue can give hope to the despondent.
>The tongue can point the way to God.

A Power for Good and Evil

The tongue, of course, has negative power as well as positive power. The Bible compares the tongue to the rudder of a ship, which, although tiny, controls the direction of the entire vessel: "Take ships as an example. Although they are so large and are driven by strong winds, they are steered by a very small rudder wherever the pilot wants to go. Likewise the tongue is a small part of the body, but it makes great boasts" (James 3:4–5a).

In other words, the tongue, although small and generally out of sight, has an extraordinary potential for producing both good and evil, holiness and havoc, beauty and beastliness, delight and destruction. "Consider," says James, "what a great forest is set on fire by a small spark" (James 3:5b).

>The tongue can make or break your marriage.
>It can make your home a paradise or a desert.
>It can draw your children to you in affection or drive them away in disgust.

It can make friends or lose them.

It can defend a good cause, or allow an evil cause to go unchecked.

It can make the difference between hiring and firing.

It can heal a church or kill it.

It can attract people to Christ or turn them away.

It can honor God or curse God.

It can save potential suicides, and it can drive people to self-destruction. As Proverbs 18:21 says, "The tongue has the power of life and death."

Your reputation will, in large part, be established by how you use your tongue. Your tongue leaves a lasting impression. It labels your character. You are known more by what you say than by how you look.

Judgment and the Tongue

At the end of the age we will be judged by how we have used our tongues. Jesus said, "And I tell you this, that you must give an account on judgment day of every idle work you speak. The words you say now reflect your fate then; either you will be justified by them or you will be condemned" (Matt. 12:36–37 NLT).

The tongue reveals more about a person than almost anything else. Although for a time the tongue may cover it up, it eventually discloses the truth about character. As the mouth of a bubbling spring reveals the water's source, the human mouth reveals the soul's condition. "A good person produces good words from a good heart, and an evil person produces evil works from an evil heart" (Matt. 12:35 NLT).

Controlling the Tongue

It's not easy to train a tongue. "People can tame all kinds of animals and birds and reptiles and fish," says James, "but no one can tame the tongue. It is an uncontrollable evil, full of deadly poison" (James 3:7–8 NLT). The tongue is an ornery critter, wild as a bucking bronco. Just when we think we have it under control—its mighty energy harnessed, its reckless nature tamed—the wild mustang spirit busts loose and the snorting creature begins bucking. Its harness dangles while its hooves fly, splintering boards and kicking up a choking dust.

How, then, can the tongue be brought under control? How can it be tamed and trained to become a thing of beauty and a useful power?

Jesus promised, "You will receive power when the Holy Spirit comes on you" (Acts 1:8). When the Spirit came at Pentecost, its first objective on earth was the tongue! The disciples spoke in languages that could be understood by the foreign Jews who were visiting in Jerusalem for the feast. Simon Peter—the same Peter who earlier had used his tongue to curse, swear, and then to deny Christ—gave a sermon, and the Holy Spirit used Peter's tongue so marvelously that three thousand people responded and were saved.

In 1 Corinthians 12:3 we read, "Therefore I tell you that no one who is speaking by the Spirit of God says, 'Jesus be cursed,' and no one can say, 'Jesus is Lord,' except by the Holy Spirit." It is the Spirit that transforms a cursing tongue into a confessing tongue.

Isaiah 6:1–8 relates the story of God preparing Isaiah for service. First, Isaiah was given a vision of God's awesome holiness, and then God sanctified Isaiah's tongue. Isaiah had realized, after his glimpse of divine power and purity, that his tongue needed to be purified. "'Woe to me!' I cried. 'I am ruined! For I am a man of unclean lips, and I live among a people of unclean lips'" (v. 5). Then the angel touched the prophet's lips with a burning coal taken from the fire. It was a sign of forgiveness and restoration —and perhaps a hint about how painful it is to cleanse the tongue. "With it he touched my mouth and said, 'See, this has touched your lips; your guilt is taken away and your sin atoned for'" (v. 7). Then, and only then, was Isaiah ready for service: "'Here am I. Send me!' And he said, 'Go'" (vv. 8b–9).

Two significant truths are illustrated in these verses: (1) when we become aware of the holiness of God, we become aware of how desperately our tongues need to be cleansed; and (2) to get ready to serve, we must let God cleanse our tongues.

Our tongues cannot become a thing of beauty by our own efforts alone. Enhancing the tongue takes the superhuman work of God's Spirit. But this does not mean that our own efforts are not needed. God has given each of us a mind and a will, and he expects us to use them. God requires that we assume responsibility for the marvelous instrument he has given us. When it comes to using the tongue, God has revealed a wealth of information and advice, and he expects us to use it.

Beautifying the tongue will be the subject of this study.

Beauty Exercises
To Help Make You a Truly Attractive Person

1. In addition to reading this lesson material and doing other exercises the group leader may suggest, you are asked to commit to memory one Scripture verse each week. Although Scripture memorization may not be the "in" thing right now, remember what the psalm writer said: "I have hidden your word in my heart that I might not sin against you" (Ps. 119:11).

    The verses for memorization will be printed at the end of each lesson under the section "Breath Fresheners." In the same way that you take mints along in your pocket or purse to sweeten your breath, take these verses with you to sweeten your words. Carrying flash cards wherever you go is a good way to aid memorization. If you are studying this book in a class, your leader may ask that you repeat the verses in unison at the meeting.

2. Carefully study chapters 3 and 4 of the book of James. They contain the most sustained treatment on the subject of the tongue in the Bible. Jot down all the items to which the tongue is compared (a horse's bit, a rudder, and so on). What is the significance of each of these analogies?

3. Reexamine your concept of beauty or handsomeness. What are you striving for most—inward attractiveness or outward attractiveness? Which

kind of beauty is more important in the eyes of the people you know and respect?

4. Include in your prayers a few sincere petitions for that important piece of flesh that lies between your teeth. Recognize that it is the Holy Spirit who can give it both discipline and power. Begin to yield your tongue to that Spirit.

Breath Fresheners
Choice Tidbits to Chew On and Digest

First: The tongue has the power of life and death. (Prov. 18:21)

Second: I am a man of unclean lips, and I live among a people of unclean lips. (Isa. 6:5)

Third: Likewise the tongue is a small part of the body, but it makes great boasts. Consider what a great forest is set on fire by a small spark. (James 3:5)

Fourth: We all make many mistakes, but those who control their tongues can also control themselves in every other way. (James 3:2 NLT)

A Beautiful Tongue Is a Silent Tongue

It was once said of a great linguist that he could remain silent in seven languages.

The Bible certainly isn't silent about the art of keeping silent.

Proverbs 10:19 says "When words are many, sin is not absent, but he who holds his tongue is wise."

Ecclesiastes states in the well-known "a time to" passage that there is "a time to be silent and a time to speak" (Eccl. 3:7). All too often we get our times mixed up; we speak when we ought to keep silent, and we keep silent when we ought to speak.

Psalm 4:4 teaches us that "when you are on your beds, search your hearts and be silent."

And it says in the letter of James, "Everyone should be quick to listen, slow to speak and slow to become angry" (James 1:19). Most of us are inclined to be just the opposite. We are slow to hear and quick to speak.

Often when we converse with another person, we don't really listen to what that person is saying. In fact, while the other person is speaking, we are thinking about what we are going to say in return. If both individuals are going through the same little ritual, we have the ludicrous situation of two people talking to themselves together! There is a sobering proverb: "Fools have no interest in understanding; they only want to air their own opinions" (Prov. 18:2 NLT).

To help develop a beautiful tongue, each of us could *initiate a program of constructive silence*. It won't be easy, because it takes more muscle power to silence the tongue than to activate it. But there is much to be gained.

Constructive Silence Eliminates Gossip

We ought to be "slow to speak" said James (1:19). Why? Because much of what we are tempted to say has no constructive purpose. Much of our talk is just gossip— a mixture of truth, half-truth, and outright untruth—that hurts everyone and helps no one. Even if what we speak is the truth, are we under an obligation to broadcast it to the world?

If we say nothing, no one can repeat it. When it comes to gossip, a beautiful tongue is a silent tongue. We'll come back to the subject of gossip in Beauty Hint 7.

Constructive Silence Promotes Harmony with Others

We would avoid a lot of trouble if we relaxed our tongue more often. James 1:19 links speech and anger.

Everyone should be "slow to speak and slow to become angry." A hot head and a quick tongue go together.

We speak most impulsively when we are angry. We speak most rapidly when we are angry. We speak most unthinkingly when we are angry. Tempers and voices rise together. It's not differences of opinion that cause hurt—it's the words said in haste during them.

In addition, we irritate people when we talk too much. Compulsive talkers find it difficult to keep friends. The good listener is more popular than the poor listener. It is simply common sense and good manners to refrain from monopolizing the conversation.

Constructive Silence Helps Hide Ignorance!

There is an old saying—"By saying nothing, one may pass as wise"—that was perhaps inspired by Proverbs 17:28: "Even fools are thought to be wise when they keep silent; when they keep their mouths shut, they seem intelligent" (NLT).

When you don't know what you're talking about, it's better to hide your ignorance than to prove it beyond reasonable doubt!

Constructive Silence Can Give You a Ministry to Others

You can help others by simply being a sounding board. People who are troubled or lonely, who are making a decision or simply need someone to care about them often need someone to talk to. You don't have to give sage advice or words of wisdom; you need only provide an open ear. You don't even have to quote Scripture. Some verses, even a great one like "we know that in all things God works for the good of those who love him" (Rom. 8:28) can sound smug and unfeeling when a person is suffering intense pain.

Some psychiatrists admit that a major part of therapy is simply listening while patients speak their minds. Clients are willing to pay big bucks to have someone listen without interrupting or arguing. Perhaps the people at home aren't willing to silence their tongues long enough to open their ears.

Church members often go to their pastors simply because they need someone who will listen. Pastors tell of parishioners who have expressed thanks over and over again for "how much you've helped" when the pastor has hardly said a word during the entire call.

Often extramarital affairs originate, not because of unfulfilled passion or premeditated unfaithfulness, but because one person needed to talk, and a friend was willing to listen. Husband and wives—listen!

Many of our personal problems could be solved or eased if we just learned to listen. We could save thousands of dollars on medical bills, enjoy happier marriages, and contribute to the well-being of others just by closing our mouths and opening our ears.

Constructive Silence Is Important in Our Relationship with God

Elijah expected God to reveal himself in the great windstorm, in the earthquake, and in the fire. Instead, God revealed himself with a gentle whisper (1 Kings 19:9–18). If Elijah hadn't kept quiet and listened intently, he wouldn't have heard God's message for him and for Israel.

"Be still," says the Lord, "and know that I am God" (Ps. 46:10). "Be still before the LORD, all humanity," said the prophet Zechariah (Zech. 2:13 NLT).

Prayer is intended to be a two-way conversation with God. Prayer uses the ears as well as the mouth. If you ask God for guidance, open the ears of your soul to hear that guidance. Listen for the gentle whisper of the divine. Give God a chance to get in a word or two—and give him enough room so he doesn't have to get those words in edgewise.

Beauty Exercises
To Help Relax Your Tongue

1. Make a call on an elderly person and give him or her an entire hour to talk about anything he or she wants to.
2. After conversing with a friend, jot down as accurately as possible everything the friend said. In other words, check on how good you were as a listener.
3. Refrain from passing on a tempting tidbit of gossip, even though you think it won't hurt anyone. Restraint is good discipline for the tongue—and the tidbit probably would have hurt someone!
4. Listen carefully at the next discussion group you attend—whether it be a Sunday school

class, a meeting of the book club, a Bible study, or whatever. What percentage of the group members did 80 percent of the talking? Were the ones who knew the most the ones who talked the most?

5. Next time you pray, give God equal time. If you pray for five minutes, remain silent for five minutes. If you pray for ten minutes, listen for ten minutes. After you have spoken to God, let God speak to you.

6. Resist the temptation to argue an unimportant point, even though you know you are right. Just be quiet about it and talk about something constructive instead. Or better yet, let somebody else talk about something constructive.

Breath Fresheners
Verses That May Have a Paralyzing Effect on the Tongue

First: Everyone should be quick to listen, slow to speak and slow to become angry. (James 1:19)

Second: Fools have no interest in understanding; they only want to air their own opinions. (Prov. 18:2 NLT)

Third: Be still before the LORD, all humanity. (Zech. 2:13 NLT)

Fourth: [There is] a time to be silent and a time to speak. (Eccl. 3:7)

A Beautiful Tongue Is an Appreciative Tongue

We all know how wonderful it is to be appreciated—to know that your love, sweat, worry, time, and tears have had a positive effect on someone, and to have that someone respond with genuine thanks.

And if it is important to *be appreciated,* then it is important to *appreciate.* It is, in fact, appreciative people who are most appreciated.

An appreciative tongue is so important in North America that we set aside a special day in October (Canada) or November (United States) to exercise it. The Pilgrims knew the value of an appreciative tongue. May we never abandon that part of our rich heritage!

An Appreciative Tongue Exemplifies True Godliness

One characteristic of genuine godliness is sincere appreciation expressed to the Almighty.

What, according to the first chapter of Romans, is the tragic fault of those who drift away from God? "For although they knew God, they neither glorified him as God nor gave thanks to him" (v. 21).

Having refused to humbly acknowledge the Creator, they further insulted God by making animalistic images of him (vv. 22–23). Then they degraded themselves by indulging their bodies in immorality (vv. 24–27). But the root of these practices was thanklessness.

God's greatest people have been appreciative people. King David addressed scores of his psalms to the theme of thankfulness (see Pss. 35:18; 65:1; 92:1; 108:1; 116:17). Paul began most of his letters with a statement of thanks (Rom. 1:8; 1 Cor. 1:4; Eph. 1:15–16) and also singled out certain people, such as Priscilla and Aquila (Rom. 16:3–4) and Onesiphorus (2 Tim. 1:16–18), for special words of appreciation.

An Appreciative Tongue Establishes a Personal Relationship with the Giver

Most of us recall the story in Luke 17:11–19 about the ten lepers healed by Jesus, only one of whom returned to give thanks. The nine who went on their way without so much as a backward glance received a blessing—that of physical healing. But the one with the appreciative tongue received an additional blessing. Not only was he healed—he got to know the Healer. Not only did he feel the power—he became personally acquainted with the source of that power. He found out that the provider was also the Savior. He was healed not only in body but also in soul.

In this story of the ten lepers we see the difference between genuine gratitude and just "feeling lucky." Doubtless, the nine who hurried off to conduct their own affairs felt lucky. One can feel lucky all by one's self, without communication and without love for anyone. Appreciation always implies communication and a person-to-person relationship. Appreciation implies a bond of friendship, and it indicates that a relationship is highly valued. Thus, gratitude to God is important; it indicates a personal relationship between the individual and God.

An Appreciative Tongue Will Put Your Requests into Perspective

> Do not be anxious about anything, but in everything, by prayer and petition, with thanksgiving, present your requests to God. (Phil. 4:6)

A beautiful prayer will not only ask God for something new; it will thank God for something old. A prayer *of* blessing will accompany a prayer *for* blessing.

If you ask God for cake, first thank him for bread. If you ask for victory over the power of sin, offer thanks for deliverance from the guilt of sin. If you pray for a happier home life, give thanks for your home. It's fine to ask God for shoes, but also thank him for feet.

An Appreciative Tongue Will Give You a Better Family Life

The woman described so glowingly in Proverbs 31 had the good fortune to be appreciated: "Her children arise and call her blessed; her husband also, and he praises her" (v. 28). No wonder she was such a remarkable person. She had a cheering section! The habit of appreciation could be found in her home.

An appreciative tongue acts as a love bond for all relationships, and that is especially true in our homes. "Thank you" is almost as important as "I love you."

Do you really want to make your spouse feel that he or she is someone special? Then appreciate him or her and express that appreciation!

Accentuate the positive. Instead of complaining about what you don't have, let your spouse know that you appreciate what you do have. The art of thanksgiving is the art of positive reinforcement. Your spouse will handle finances more responsibly if you compliment what he or she does right. Your spouse will be a better lover if you verbalize your pleasure. Your spouse will become a better parent if you praise the way he or she handled a particular situation.

Loved ones tend to become what you say they are.

An Appreciative Tongue Can Change Your Perspective on Things

The person who has learned to appreciate has learned to see the beautiful.

A vulture and a hummingbird are flying over the same desert. The vulture will find a decaying carcass. The hummingbird will find a beautiful flower. They will find what they are looking for. We will find what we expect to find.

The appreciative grocery customer will notice the friendliness of the bagger rather than the grumpiness of the cashier. The appreciative gardener will be happy over the strawberries rather than disgusted with the weeds. An appreciative parent will talk more about the joy of seeing the child grow than about the distastefulness of dirty diapers. The appreciative person will treasure neighbors' friendliness instead of complaining about their noisy dog. The appreciative person will treasure the truth of the sermon rather than deploring the preacher's nasal tone.

An Appreciative Tongue Can Strengthen Your Character

Appreciation leads to imitation. We tend to become what we admire.

The person who appreciates generosity in others is likely to become generous. The person who appreciates beautiful art is more likely to create his or her own beautiful art. The person who compliments another for a job well done is more likely to be a careful and faithful worker. The person who appreciates Jesus Christ for his self-giving love is more likely to adopt Jesus as a role model.

An Appreciative Tongue Can Brighten the Day for Someone

You know the feeling—everything seems to be going wrong, or you feel depressed, or you wonder if what you've done is worth the effort. Then, without warning, someone—be it a friend, family member, or stranger—makes an appreciative comment on how you look, or how well you did the job, or how you handled a certain situation. That comment makes all the difference in the world. If a word of appreciation can brighten your day, you can be sure it will have the same effect on someone else. So go immediately to Beauty Exercise 1 below.

Beauty Exercises
To Help You Express Your Appreciation

1. During the next week compliment five or more of the following people, taking note of their responses (your group leader may ask you to report on this at the next meeting):
   a. the checkout person at a supermarket, for having a pleasant smile
   b. the server at a restaurant, for being efficient and polite
   c. a Sunday school teacher, for being faithful and interesting
   d. the organist, for an excellent prelude (If you really want to shock him or her, make a nice comment about the postlude; no one ever seems to listen to that.)

    e. a neighbor, for a neatly trimmed lawn and beautiful flowers

    f. a fellow worker, for doing the job right

    g. your husband, for having an uncanny ability to fix the toaster

    h. or—your wife, for having an uncanny ability to fix the toaster

    i. your mother-in-law, for her excellent gravy

2. When you pray, accompany each request with a related word of thanks. Discipline yourself not to ask for anything until you have first thanked God for something.

3. Look for things to be thankful for rather than for things to gripe about. Be like the hummingbird, not the vulture. You may discover a treasury of beauty, love, and strength that you never knew was there.

4. Write a letter of appreciation to someone who has contributed to your life. You've thought about it before but have never gotten around to it, so don't put it off any longer!

5. Read Psalms 90 and 106.

6. Choose a person who seems to dislike you. Surprise him or her with a word of appreciation.

Breath Fresheners
Don't You Wish Everybody Did?

    First: Give thanks to the Lord, for he is good; his love endures forever. (Ps. 107:1)

Second: Do not be anxious about anything, but in everything, by prayer and petition, with thanksgiving, present your requests to God. (Phil. 4:6)

Third: For everything God created is good, and nothing is to be rejected if it is received with thanksgiving. (1 Tim. 4:4)

Fourth: Give thanks in all circumstances, for this is God's will for you in Christ Jesus. (1 Thess. 5:18)

A Beautiful Tongue Is a Witnessing Tongue

There are two extremes when it comes to witnessing for Christ. Some cannot hold a normal conversation without making a hard-sell pitch for salvation. Soon others avoid them as if they had bad breath.

On the other hand are people who never, never, ever give the slightest indication that they are Christians and wouldn't have the foggiest idea what to say if asked how to become one.

Most of us probably fall somewhere between these two extremes. A few of us perhaps should tone down a bit, but most of us are closer to the second extreme than to the first. We talk about our church, but we don't talk much about our faith. We talk about our minister, but we don't say much about our Savior. We pass up glorious opportunities to witness, because we are afraid of what people might say—and because we are afraid that we don't know what to say.

A Private Faith Must Also Be a Public Faith

Believing and confessing are twins. What the heart knows the tongue must say. "If you confess with your mouth, 'Jesus is Lord,' and believe in your heart that God raised him from the dead, you will be saved" (Rom. 10:9). Christ needs public defenders more than he needs secret disciples.

The short sentence "Jesus is Lord" is apparently the earliest Christian creed and was used by believers even before the so-called Apostles' Creed. It doesn't contain a lot of scholarly theology; it can simply be a personal statement of what Jesus means to the speaker—he is the Lord of my life, and he is my Lord because he is, first of all, my Savior.

A Witnessing Tongue Is Not "For Professionals Only"

As a church we hire a "professional" to do our witnessing so we won't have to do it. We help pay the bills, and our conscience is clear.

But there is a problem. The "professional" doesn't usually travel where we travel, doesn't meet the people we meet, doesn't mingle where we mingle, doesn't work where we work. The "professional," in fact, has the disadvantage of being perceived as someone who gets paid to promote religion and sign up new members. To a non-believer, though, the difference between hearing the Good News from a "professional" or hearing it from you is like the difference between a vacuum cleaner salesman saying, "This is the best vacuum cleaner on the market" and a neighbor saying, "I bought one of those vacuum cleaners last year and I really like it."

A Witnessing Tongue Shares a Personal Faith

> Always be prepared to give . . . the reason
> for the hope that you have. (1 Peter 3:15)

Peter's statement presupposes a life beaming with hope, a life so unique that it causes people to say, "I wonder what makes him [or her] so happy." If your mood is grumpy and morose, if your tongue is critical and nasty, no one is going to call on you "to give the reason for the hope that you have." A beautiful life and a beautiful tongue must be combined in order to make a beautiful witness.

The context for sharing the reason for one's hope is not just the church—the safe and sympathetic body of believers, the riskless gathering of kindred spirits. The context is the marketplace, the office, the factory, the lunchroom, the bowling alley, the book club, the carpool, the classroom, the lounge, the service organization.

First Peter 3:15 gives us three important characteristics of a beautiful witnessing tongue.

A Witnessing Tongue Is a Prepared Tongue

First of all, a witnessing tongue is a *prepared* tongue. Your tongue, said Peter, must "always be prepared" to give the reason for your hope.

Being prepared means being willing. That's the opposite of hesitant, embarrassed, reluctant. Being prepared means that, even in an unfriendly atmosphere, you won't be tempted to hedge, fudge, cover up, deny, or play down your convictions.

Being prepared means being eager—actually to want to talk about your faith, to be enthusiastic about what Christ has done for you, and to be positive about your experience as a member of Christ's church.

Being prepared also means giving forethought to what you are going to say. You don't have to take a seminary course or graduate from an evangelism program, but it is important to know the basic principles of the Christian faith, and it's helpful to think through the personal stories you want to tell. Many growing congregations offer classes on witnessing that include step-by-step procedures, Scripture verses to memorize, and practical experience in sharing one's faith.

A Witnessing Tongue Is a Gentle Tongue

Secondly, the witnessing tongue must be a *gentle* tongue. "But do this with gentleness," said Peter. The witnessing tongue must reflect the compassionate spirit of Christ as he dealt with various kinds of people in his day.

The witnessing tongue must attract rather than antagonize, invite rather than threaten, share rather than preach, and console rather than condemn. If the bridge of human friendship is blocked, the gospel will not get across. Seldom, if ever, has anyone been argued into the kingdom.

A Witnessing Tongue Is a Respectful Tongue

Peter added a third criteria for effectively sharing your faith: "But do this with gentleness *and respect.*" Respect is related to gentleness but goes a step farther; it holds in esteem the personality of the other person. It tries to connect with the other person at the point of their training and background. It seeks to understand his or her doubts, animosities, and hesitancies. It respects convictions, tries to understand, and acknowledges the right to differ. And— a witnessing tongue does not get into political debates.

A Witnessing Tongue Relies on the Holy Spirit

While training, self-confidence, and competence are important, we must ultimately trust in the power of the Holy Spirit to help us be effective witnesses. One person can plant, said Paul, and another can water, but only God can produce the harvest (see 1 Cor. 3:6–7). Our most eloquent recitals will fall on deaf ears without the help of the Holy Spirit.

Jesus had comforting words for disciples who were soon to feel unprepared and alone in a hostile world: "But when they arrest you, do not worry about what to say or how to say it. At that time you will be given what to say, for it will not be you speaking, but the Spirit of your Father speaking through you" (Matt. 10:19).

We cannot possibly be prepared for every situation, but we need not fear the unknown. There are times when our best-learned techniques must be abandoned, when our careful plans must be thrown aside, and when we will hear ourselves speaking words that are completely spontaneous and unrehearsed. It is God's Holy Spirit that gives power to the witnessing tongue.

Beauty Exercises
For a Tongue That Shares Hope

1. Become involved in congregational outreach. Your involvement may be as ambitious as becoming an evangelistic caller or as simple as stuffing envelopes for a community mailing—but *do something.*
2. Talk to your pastor about the outreach ministry of your congregation. Help your pastor to evaluate strengths and weaknesses, point out needs, and encourage efforts to initiate new approaches. And yes—offer your services.
3. Make a list of people you wish to invite to come to church. Now call up the first person or family on that list and invite them to come with you this Sunday.

4. Invite a new Christian for coffee, a meal, or a social event. Be ready to talk about your own faith journey, being honest about your struggles as well as your triumphs. Friendship and support are very important.

5. Think through your personal journey of faith. What stories from your life experience would be helpful when shared with others? What personal struggles could encourage others? What past incidents in your life are clear evidences of God's activity?

6. Try to establish a genuine friendship with a person who is not a Christian believer—perhaps a coworker, a neighbor, a golf partner, or a fellow "soccer mom." Get to know this person and establish a rapport that will encourage a mutual sharing of convictions. This friendship, however, should not be manipulative; don't look at the other person as an object of witness only, to be abandoned if your testimony is not accepted.

Breath Fresheners
To Add a Hint of More Than Mint

First: If you confess with your mouth, "Jesus is Lord," and believe in your heart that God raised him from the dead, you will be saved. (Rom. 10:9)

Second: Always be prepared to give an answer to everyone who asks you to give the reason for the hope that you have. But do this with gentleness and respect. (1 Peter 3:15b)

Third: I am not ashamed of the gospel. (Rom. 1:16a)

Fourth: Go and make disciples of all nations. . . . And surely I am with you always, to the very end of the age. (Matt. 28:19a, 20b)

A Beautiful Tongue Is a Clean Tongue

A toothpaste manufacturer claims that its product is effective when used with a "conscientiously applied program of oral hygiene."

What our country needs is a conscientiously applied program of oral hygiene. And it's not the kind that comes out of a toothpaste tube or involves visiting your dentist twice a year. It's the kind that only Christ can give when he applies his unique cleansing action to the entire oral cavity.

North America has an X-rated mouth. Profanity is everywhere:

- from the inner city to the suburbs
- from the loading dock to the vice president's office
- from the PTA to the senate
- from the locker room to the business convention
- from the family room to the boot camp

- from the movie screen to the Broadway stage
- from the school yard to the bowling alley

There was a time when men excused themselves if they used profanity in the presence of a woman. Now they feel they don't have to.

There Is a Pollution That Poisons

We're concerned about air pollution, water pollution, and earth pollution. We also ought to be concerned about the pollution of the sound waves.

The words of Jesus are appropriate to a generation that worries about the purity of what we eat, breathe, and drink: "You are not defiled by what you eat; you are defiled by what you say and do" (Matt. 15:11 NLT).

"But why," you might ask, "should profanity be considered bad? It really doesn't hurt anybody. It's my own business what I say and how I say it." That's what people used to say about air pollution. But experience has shown that pollution's long-term effects—although not always apparent—can be serious in the long run. Toxins have a habit of seeping into the brain and the soul, poisoning the inner depths of one's being and polluting the streams of society.

Enough about a dirty tongue; let's talk about the beauty of a clean tongue.

A Clean Tongue Shows Reverence for God

> You shall not misuse the name of the LORD
> your God, for the LORD will not hold anyone
> guiltless who misuses his name. (Exod. 20:7)

Society may regard abusing God's name as harmless and perhaps even cute. But the Bible says that God will not hold guiltless those who misuse his name.

A name is more than just a name. A name represents a person. When Sally Smith bitterly complains that she has "lost her good name," she is not saying that someone has harmed the letters SALLY SMITH. She is saying that someone has harmed her reputation, besmirched her character, and hurt her to the core of her being.

Similarly, to misuse the name of God is to misuse more than a few letters of the alphabet. It is to misuse a Person. It is to show extreme disrespect for the Holy One. It is to harm God's reputation. It is to attack God's very being. It is to play lightly with God's character.

To use God's name carefully, however, and only in the proper context is to show reverence, respect, honor, and love for the One that name represents. "Ascribe to the LORD the glory due his name," said the psalm writer (Ps. 29:2). "This, then, is how you should pray," said Jesus, "'Our Father in heaven, hallowed be your name'" (Matt. 6:9).

A Clean Tongue Displays Reverence for All Things: Holy, Personal, Private, and Significant

The vast majority of swear words fall into two general categories—God and sex. Thus, swear words cheapen two of the most significant, personal, and intimate relationships of our lives—those that concern our spiritual lives and our love lives. The profane tongue implies contempt and low esteem.

Profanity has been called "verbal pornography," and the results of the verbal kind can be just as damaging as the results of the visual kind.

A clean tongue is a beautiful tongue, because it articulates reverence for all things good and beautiful, reverence for life itself, reverence for the way God made us, reverence for the bodies of the ones we love, and reverence for our own bodies—each of which is a "temple of the Holy Spirit" (1 Cor. 6:19). Those who speak with a clean tongue express a sensitivity to the spiritual. Those who speak with a clean tongue express a high esteem for one's most intimate and loving relationship. "Nor should there be," said Paul, "obscenity, foolish talk or coarse joking, which are out of place, but rather thanksgiving" (Eph. 5:4).

A Clean Tongue Displays Good Stewardship of the God-Given Talent of Clear, Concise, and Colorful Speech

A fundamental rule of effective communication is to avoid hackneyed, trite, and overused phrases.

The most hackneyed, trite, overused, and unoriginal words in the English language are swear words. When was the last time you heard a new one? If the use of trite language identifies an amateur writer, profanity identifies an amateur talker. It takes no creativity, brains, originality, special talent, or even thought to use cuss words. A parrot or myna bird can be taught to swear. Even if profanity were spiritually and ethically acceptable, it would be an inferior form of communication.

The ability to communicate by means of the tongue is one of God's greatest gifts. The Christian believer realizes that speech, like other talents and abilities, is to be used and perfected as part of one's total stewardship.

God has given us wonderful powers of communication; let us use them as creatively, forcefully, and clearly as we can.

A Clean Tongue Indicates Our Ability to Deal Appropriately with the Frustrations of Life

Our verbal responses reveal our capacity for exasperation. Cursing has been called a "nuclear fly swatter," since it is usually out of proportion to the situation. The same words are used whether one hits a thumb with a hammer, sees one's home in flames, or misses a two-foot putt. A clean tongue indicates our ability to cope in a mature manner with the traumas and inconveniences of life.

A Clean Tongue Reveals a Pure Heart

The things that come out of the mouth, said Jesus, come from the heart (Matt. 15:18). Our language reveals our inner resources. It reveals our basic attitudes toward our bodies, love, other people, Christ, God, and life in general. Profanity may reveal a serious problem with the soul, and a clean tongue may very well reveal a heart that is right with God through Jesus Christ, a heart cleansed and empowered by the power of the Holy Spirit.

A Clean Tongue Is, by Its Very Rarity, a Witnessing Tongue

Profanity is so common today that its very absence is distinctive. People who have clean tongues stand out in a group simply because they are a rarity.

It can be hoped that one's Christian witness will be more explicit than the mere absence of gutter words, but a clean tongue will go a long way towards demonstrating a person's integrity and convictions. Others will suspect that you are a Christian and may even begin to excuse or curtail their own foul speech in your presence.

Beauty Exercises

To Include in Your Conscientiously Applied Program of Oral Hygiene

1. Are you memorizing your "Breath Fresheners"? Remember also to review all the verses you've learned.

2. If your children use vulgar or profane language, don't allow it to go undisciplined and unchecked. The old "washing-the-mouth-out-with-soap treatment" may sound silly, but it works!

3. Incidentally, check to see where your children are learning those words. Could it be in your own home?

4. Remember to forget the smutty story you heard yesterday.

Breath Fresheners
To Keep Your Breath Clean

First: You shall not misuse the name of the LORD your God, for the LORD will not hold anyone guiltless who misuses his name. (Exod. 20:7)

Second: I am the LORD; that is my name! I will not give my glory to another. (Isa. 42:8)

Third: The things that come out of the mouth come from the heart. (Matt. 15:18)

Fourth: Do not let any unwholesome talk come out of your mouths, but only what is helpful for building others up. (Eph. 4:29)

A Beautiful Tongue Is a Kind Tongue

One of the most familiar chapters of the Bible begins with these words: "If I speak in the tongues of men and of angels, but have not love, I am only a resounding gong or a clanging cymbal" (1 Cor. 13:1).

Cymbals have their place in an orchestra, but can you imagine the distraction if they clanged constantly throughout an entire symphony?

Clanging gongs have their place in life—to wake us up, to warn us of fire, and to tell students that a period is over—but when the bell "sticks," the sound becomes deafening and irritating.

Such is the sound of a voice without kindness. It may speak with beautiful eloquence, perfect diction, erudite intelligence, and syrupy sweetness. It may even speak in unknown tongues. But if it does not speak with genuine love, it only emits a grating sound of aggravating disharmony.

Jesus taught that the entire Law can be summarized in one word—love. "Love the Lord. . . . Love your neighbor" (Mark 12:30–31). A person who speaks with love is keeping both the content and the spirit of the Ten Commandments. The person who speaks kindly has made good progress in keeping God's holy law.

A Kind Tongue Helps Make a House a Home

Proverbs 31 is a remarkable and still-timely vignette about a truly wonderful wife and mother. She is faithful, ambitious, skilled, intelligent, and generous. But she is more than that: she is kind. The beauty of her person is enhanced by the kindness of her words. "She speaks with wisdom, and faithful instruction is on her tongue" (Prov. 31:26). It is no wonder, then, that a few verses later it says, "Her children arise and call her blessed; her husband also, and he praises her" (v. 28).

The place to begin with kindness, as with most good things, is at home.

Many, if not most, family problems could be solved or at least eased by a kind tongue. A little kindness goes a long way when your wife or husband comes home from work, hot, tired, and irritable. A little kindness can solve a lot of math problems when Junior becomes disgusted with his homework. A little kindness dries many tears when Sally comes home crying because she's "so ugly."

A Kind Tongue Overcomes Speech Problems

Some people feel self-conscious when they speak. They think that they say "dumb things," or have a peculiar accent, or have a voice that it pitched too high or too low, or have a limited vocabulary, or say the wrong thing at the wrong time.

If you feel this way, the accent of kindness may do more for you than a college course in public speaking. If you speak in love, all the imperfections (supposed or real) simply become a harmony to the melody of kindness.

A Kind Tongue Supplements a Truthful Tongue

The book of Ephesians says that it's not enough to speak the truth. We are to speak the truth "in love" (Eph. 4:15).

Perhaps your husband irritates others when he cracks his knuckles in public. Tell him the truth—but tell the truth in love. Perhaps your wife irritates others when she laughs too loudly in public. Tell her the truth—but tell the truth in love.

Perhaps a friend is inviting tragedy by becoming too friendly with a coworker. Tell your friend the truth—but do so with kindness.

Perhaps the cult member who calls at your door is teaching a false and dangerous doctrine. Share your understanding of the truth with your caller—but do so in love, without nasty remarks and a slammed door.

A Kind Tongue Promotes Peace

The apostle Peter (who, by the way, had to struggle with a boisterous and unruly tongue), says, "Don't repay evil for evil. Don't retaliate when people say unkind things about you. Instead, pay them back with a blessing. That is what God wants you to do, and he will bless you for it. For the Scriptures say, 'If you want a happy life and good days, keep your tongue from speaking evil, and keep you tongue from telling lies'" (1 Peter 3:9–10 NLT).

According to the epistle of James, the tongue is like a wild horse, difficult to bridle and control. There is, however, one bit that can control the tongue—a bit (pardon the pun) of love.

We need a bit of love at all times, but we especially need it when faced with antagonism. It's easy to be kind to others when they are kind to us. The real test of kindness comes when we are provoked.

It's easy to smile at customers who are satisfied; it's harder when they blame you for high prices.

It's easy to be kind when your neighbors are pleasant and mind their own business; it's not so easy when they complain about the twigs from your trees on their lawn, or when they imply you're raising a brood of delinquents.

Jesus' kind tongue revealed that he was an extraordinary person. "When they hurled their insults at him, he did not retaliate; when he suffered, he made no threats" (1 Peter 2:23). He controlled the impulse to speak out in anger against the people who were seeking to kill him. Among his dying words were words of kindness: "Father, forgive them, for they do not know what they are doing" (Luke 23:34).

A Kind Tongue Is a Positive Witness for Christ

I know a woman who is recognized in her church as an articulate leader at women's meetings and as an impressive participant in public prayer. But those who deliver her mail and newspaper, pick up her garbage, mow her lawn, and play in the yard next door call her "Mrs.

Complainer" (although they usually use a word the editors said we couldn't print here). Despite her angelic utterances in church, she is a poor testimony to the transforming love of Jesus Christ. Her beautiful sounds are no more than clanging gongs and clashing cymbals.

The advice of Colossians 4:6 is appropriate: "Let your conversation be always full of grace, seasoned with salt."

All too often, Christians fail to accompany their moral convictions with a touch of kindness, somehow believing that kind words and smiles offered to people of differing opinions reflect a lack of conviction. We would do well to heed the bedtime prayer of one little girl: "Dear God, make more people Christians, and make more Christians nice."

Beauty Exercises
For the Development of a Kind Tongue

1. Choose a person you dislike, someone who really irritates you, then speak, call, or write to him or her, doing your best to be genuinely kind. You don't have to overact, but do exhibit a gracious and positive attitude.

2. Next time you see the person who delivers your newspaper, speak kindly to him or her, no matter how many times you have found your paper under the bushes. (A kind word may improve the carrier's aim.) Do likewise with the mail carrier, grocery store bagger, and delivery person.

3. Hold your tongue the next time someone provokes you. Try to understand why the other

person acts that way. Smother, don't fan, the potential quarrel.

4. Discuss with a few teenagers (preferably your own, if you have any) what impresses them most and what disillusions them most about adult Christians. How important are kindness and love to them?

5. Be ready to share your friendship at a church meeting.

6. Write an original paraphrase of 1 Corinthians 13:1–3. Be creative and down to earth. You might try "A Housewife's Version of 1 Corinthians 13" or "A Business Person's Version" or "A School-teacher's Version" or "A Retiree's Version."

Breath Fresheners
For a Mouth That's Always Pleasant

First: If I speak in the tongues of men and of angels, but have not love, I am only a resounding gong or a clanging cymbal. (1 Cor. 13:1)

Second: Be kind and compassionate to one another, forgiving each other, just as in Christ God forgave you. (Eph. 4:32)

Third: Let your conversation be always full of grace, seasoned with salt. (Col. 4:6)

Fourth: Speaking the truth in love, we will in all things grow up into him who is the Head, that is, Christ. (Eph. 4:15)

A Beautiful Tongue Is a Nongossiping Tongue

I have heard people confess almost every sin known to humankind, plus a few more. But I've never heard anyone admit to gossiping.

Perhaps gossiping is so common that we don't realize we are doing it. Perhaps we think we have excused ourselves by saying, "I don't mean to talk about her, but . . ." or "This is just between you and me." Perhaps we convince ourselves that we are really expressing concern for the person we are talking about. Perhaps the line between gossip and news is sometimes blurred. Perhaps if we admitted to gossiping, we would feel obligated to stop.

Gossip is one of the most subtle and common diseases of the tongue. It infects young and old, male and female, rich and poor, married and unmarried. It is highly communicable (pardon the pun), and leaves ugly scars.

A Tongue That Does Not Gossip Solves the Retrieval Problem

Letting the cat out of the bag is easy, but it's hard to get the creature back in.

Once a rumor is started, it's almost impossible to stop. We may be sorry about it and we may be forgiven by God for it, but we cannot undo the consequences. If we refuse to gossip, we solve the retrieval problem before it starts. It's easier to prevent a forest fire than to put one out.

Depend on this: The words you say about others will eventually get back to them. Ecclesiastes says, "Do not revile the king even in your thoughts, or curse the rich in your bedroom, because a bird of the air may carry your words, and a bird on the wing may report what you say" (10:20). In other words, if you defame someone it's almost certain that person will learn about it. The means may be so mysterious that we accuse the birds, but the gossip, nonetheless, gets spread.

"He who covers over an offense promotes love," says Proverbs, "but whoever repeats the matter separates close friends" (17:9).

A good rule to follow: If you wouldn't say it to someone's face, don't say it.

A Tongue That Does Not Gossip Expresses Love

We can express love for others by refusing to gossip about them. The second great commandment is to love our neighbor as ourselves (Matt. 22:39). Even if the tales we spread pass the test of truth, they still must pass the test of love.

According to 1 Corinthians 13, one of the characteristics of love is that it "does not delight in evil but rejoices with the truth" (13:6). Phillips translates the passage this way: "It does not keep account of evil or gloat over the wickedness of other people. On the contrary, it is glad with all good men when truth prevails." The *New English Bible* sheds still further light: "Love keeps no score of wrongs; does not gloat over other men's sins, but delights in the truth."

A substantial part of gossip is gloating over the sins, faults, misfortunes, and idiosyncrasies of other people. Love, according to the Word, denies that luxury to our egos. We express our love to others by telling good news about them and refraining from wallowing in the bad.

What does the Bible say we should do when a fellow believer falls into sin? Does it say we should spread the news all over town? Note Galatians 6:1: "Dear friends, if a brother or sister is overcome by some sin, you who are godly should gently and humbly help that person back onto the right path. And be careful not to fall into the same temptation yourself" (NLT).

We Can Overcome Gossip by Developing Healthy Self-Respect

When we feel insecure and threatened we are tempted to spread ugly stories about others. By rubbing some of the glitter from some else's crown, we believe our own crown will shine more brightly. By cutting others down, we think we will stand taller. As someone has said, "To speak ill of others is only a round-about way of bragging about yourself."

The solution, then, is not merely to stop downgrading others but also to develop a healthy self-respect. Jesus said, "Love your neighbor as yourself" (Matt. 22:39). He didn't say *instead* of yourself. He said *as* yourself. He implied that we can't really accept our neighbors until we accept ourselves. And we can accept ourselves because God has accepted us, creating us in his own image, sending his Son to die for us, promising the power of the Spirit for us, and preparing a place for us to live with him forever.

We Can Overcome Gossip by Stimulating Our Minds

Charles Allen said in *God's Psychiatry* (Revell, 1953, p. 75), "Those of great minds discuss ideas, people of mediocre minds discuss events, and those of small minds discuss other people."

One positive solution to gossip is to involve your mind with better and more important things. Inform yourself about the ideological issues of the day. Keep up with world events and their significance. Read good books—nonfiction as well as fiction. Flip the television dial from a sitcom or soap opera to a good debate, documentary, or talk show (yes, there are a few intelligent ones left!). Take an interest in the great social challenges of our time, such as race, peace, and poverty, and be able to discuss them intelligently.

We Can Overcome Gossip by Keeping Busy

The housewife has made the beds and washed the dishes. It's not yet time to make lunch, and the soap operas don't come on until afternoon, so she spends an hour on the phone with a friend—talking about you-know-who.

The retiree has pulled all the weeds, and the mail won't be here for three hours, so he seeks out a neighbor for a cup of coffee and the latest news.

These are not new situations. Paul observed that widows in the church often did not have enough to do, so "not only do they become idlers, but also gossips and busybodies" (1 Tim. 5:13).

One of the best cures for gossip is to get busy doing something constructive so that you don't have time to worry about the private business of others.

We Can Overcome Gossip by Recognizing That It Has Become Habitual

Many students who have been away at college are shocked when they return home—shocked at the intensity and volume of their parents' gossip. When living at home they had simply accepted gossip as normal, but now that they have been away for a while they see it from a new perspective. Perhaps a tape recorder placed in the kitchen or family room would shock us into realizing how pervasive gossip can become.

We Can Overcome "Christian Corporate Gossip" by Checking Things Out

Over the last several decades the Christian community has been guilty of spreading several rumors that might be categorized as "corporate gossip."

One such rumor is that "Madalyn Murray O'Hair is at it again," trying to get all Christian programming off the airwaves. Since 1974, concerned Christians have spent millions of dollars sending millions of petitions to the

Federal Communications Commission (FCC), and the FCC has spent millions of dollars answering every letter. The whole thing is a complete fabrication. On July 24, 1976, *TV Guide* ran an article, "The Curse of the Phantom Petition," but the phantom lives on. O'Hair is "not at it again" and has, in fact, for several years been missing and presumed dead. In the meantime, Christians have made fools of themselves and of their faith.

Another bit of Christian corporate gossip is that the logo of Proctor and Gamble is a satanic symbol and that a Proctor and Gamble executive admitted to satanism on either the Phil Donahue or the Merv Griffin television talk show. Again, the story had no basis in fact, but many in the Christian community began boycotting Proctor and Gamble products solely on the strength of this gossip.

Beauty Exercises
Designed to Eliminate Excess Flap

1. Before you pass along any story, check with the subject of the story to see if it is true. If, for instance, you hear that Pat Brown is stepping out on her husband, check with Pat Brown. This should accomplish one of two things: it will either curtail your talk, or it will curtail Pat Brown's extracurricular activities.
2. Test each story you hear by Philippians 4:8:
    * Is it true?
    * Is it noble?

- Is it right?
- Is it pure?
- Is it lovely?
- Is it admirable?

If it passes all these tests, then by all means get on the telephone or Internet and pass it on!

3. Discuss the proposed cures for gossiping. Talk them over with your spouse and children.

4. Next time you are having coffee with friends, mutually agree to talk about anything except other people. Make a rule that the first offender has to pay a penalty, such as a dollar or buying sweet rolls for the next get-together. It may sound silly, but it will help keep you aware.

Breath Fresheners
For Conversations That Sparkle but Don't Burn

First: Without wood a fire goes out; without gossip a quarrel dies down. (Prov. 26:20)

Second: Whoever repeats the matter separates close friends. (Prov. 17:9b)

Third: Whatever is true, whatever is noble, whatever is right, whatever is pure, whatever is lovely, whatever is admirable—if anything is excellent or praiseworthy—think about such things. (Phil. 4:8)

Fourth: Love does not delight in evil but rejoices with the truth. (1 Cor. 13:6)

A Beautiful Tongue
Is a Truthful Tongue

A beautiful tongue is a truthful tongue because God, who invented the tongue, designed it to tell the truth. "Surely," said the psalm writer, "you desire truth in the inner parts" (Ps. 51:6). "The LORD hates those who don't keep their word," said the writer of Proverbs, "but he delights in those who do" (Prov. 12:22 NLT). The ninth commandment calls for a truthful tongue: "You shall not give false testimony against your neighbor" (Exod. 20:16).

God is such a stickler for the truth because he is a God of truth. "God is not a man, that he should lie. . . . Does he promise and not fulfill?" (Num. 23:19). The enemy, Satan, is called "a liar and the father of lies" (John 8:44). Murderers, idolaters, and others will join liars in the "fiery lake of burning sulfur" (Rev. 21:8). The lying tongue will come to a rather ugly end.

Lying is one of the worst forms of moral ugliness. A lie caused our first parents to sin in the Garden of Eden.

Lies brought about the sudden deaths of Ananias and Sapphira (Acts 5:1–11). Lies pinned Jesus to the cross.

More money is stolen by the tip of the tongue than by the point of a gun. Burglars may steal their thousands, but liars steal their tens of thousands—by padded expense accounts, misrepresented goods, falsified tax returns, altered records, false diagnosis of mechanical problems, and various confidence schemes.

There is little that breaks down the mutual confidence and respect of home life more quickly than the discovery of a lie. It says of the "wife of noble character" in Proverbs 31 that "Her husband has full confidence in her" (v. 11). Mutual trust is the silent but essential oxygen that fuels the fires of love.

Most of us avoid telling outright and blatant lies. It is the subtle untruths that keep our tongues from being as beautiful as they could be. These subtle untruths will be addressed in this discussion.

A Truthful Tongue Avoids Half-Truths

There are many ways of avoiding the truth. One of them is to tell only part of the truth. "A truck ran into my back fender at the intersection of Fourth and Grove." That's true, of course—but the other half of the truth is that the truck went through a green light and you went through a red one. "I'm late for work because the alarm didn't go off" may be true, but the other half of the truth is that I forgot to set it.

Another way to tell a half-truth is to combine truth and falsehood in one statement, thus making the falsehood more plausible. Satan used that ruse when tempting

Adam and Eve. "For God knows that when you eat of it your eyes will be opened, and you will be like God, knowing good and evil" (Gen. 3:5). That was partially correct, of course, because they would come to know evil as well as good. But the other part of the statement, that they would be like God, was a lie.

"She has been acting grumpy lately," someone may say. "She must be angry with me over something." The first part of the statement may be entirely true and the second entirely false. Yet when they are placed side by side, the false is made to sound true.

A Truthful Tongue Speaks Up to Defend the Truth

A person can tell a lie merely by keeping silent. Jesus was condemned by lies, but he also was condemned because no one stood up before Pilate to tell the truth and set the record straight.

Over coffee after a women's meeting someone speculates that since Jean Simpson has missed two meetings in a row, "she's probably mad about something again." You don't really care for Jean Simpson, and you know that she often does get angry about little things. But you also know that she's visiting a sister in Chicago. If you say nothing, you are implying consent to the unkind judgment.

A Truthful Tongue Distinguishes Between Fact and Opinion

Every day we hear opinions stated as facts. "He probably got kicked out of college for drinking." "She certainly is unfriendly." "He's a poor minister." "You can't trust him." But these statements are personal viewpoints only; they are apt to be biased and one-sided. They would be more accurately stated if preceded by "I think that . . ." Persons with a beautiful tongue have trained themselves to separate fact from implication, opinion, deduction, and innuendo.

A Truthful Tongue Is Careful About Absolutes

"Henry," she says, "you never talk to me any more." That's not quite the truth, is it? It's the kind of exaggerated statement that so often cuts to the heart.

- "You are always so ungrateful."
- "All you ever think about is sex."
- "You're just like your mother."
- "We never go out any more."
- "I don't have anything to wear."

Words like *always* and *never* are often (but not always!) the ingredients of a lie.

A Truthful Tongue Speaks the Truth About Oneself

It's perhaps (notice I used the word *perhaps*) as easy to be dishonest about oneself as to be untruthful about others.

How easily we justify our prejudices, excuse our mistakes, defend our bad judgments, and rationalize why we have failed. A teenager said after his mother had lectured him on some misdeed, "Mom, why do you suppose I act this way? Is it heredity or environment?"

On the other hand, it is an untruth to underrate ourselves. We can fail by telling ourselves a lie: "I can't do it" or "I'm not smart enough," or "People will laugh at me," or "I'll make a fool of myself."

God gave you talents, vitality, personality, and strength. Don't lie about what God gave you!

A Truthful Tongue Is Careful About "White Lies"

Most of us agree that it is almost always best to tell the truth, the whole truth, and nothing but the truth. But there are borderline cases—the "white lies" that are meant for good.

Sometimes the commandment to love takes precedence over the letter of the law. Some residents of the Netherlands, for instance, gave refuge to Jews during World War II and lied about it to the Nazis. A housewife, to protect herself, might tell a stranger at the door that her husband is napping in the next room.

But what about the husband who tells his wife that her new dress looks great on her, even when it doesn't? The parents who tell their children that Aunt Jenny went away on a long vacation, when in fact she ran off with the janitor? The family who tells a loved one that the cancer hasn't spread, when in fact the prognosis is grim?

Telling the Truth Builds Trust

White lies often produce short-term benefits and long-term problems. While the truth may sometimes cause immediate discomfort, it eventually builds confidence and trust. Yes, the truth sometimes hurts. But white lies, intended for the best, can cause even more hurt if they shield a friend or loved one from reality.

You may not be immediately popular when you tell a friend that such-and-such a hair style is not right for her, but over time you will establish a reputation as one who can be trusted to give an honest opinion. You may not be immediately popular when you say to a friend, "You really were driving too fast," but the truth may help avert tragedy.

A true friend is one who can be trusted to tell the truth.

It may be embarrassing to admit that you are late because you didn't start out on time, but in the long run you'll be more credible than if you are always being "caught in traffic," getting "stopped by a train," having "car trouble," or taking "a detour."

Telling the Truth Takes the Worry Out of Talking

When you always tell the truth you never have to worry about keeping your story straight. You never have to take up extra brain space by storing up those fictitious accounts. You'll never embarrass yourself by hearing someone say, "When I talked to you before, you told me you had been laid off because of downsizing."

Beauty Exercises
To Help Us Enjoy the Freedom Produced by Truth

1. Keep a notebook record of falsehoods, half-truths, and assorted opinions that are passed on to you as facts. Include such items as
    - what the garage man said was wrong with your car
    - the claims made by a television commercial
    - a radio preacher's statement that his interpretation of some obscure passage in the prophecy of Ezekiel was the only one possible
    - the excuses your children give for not practicing the piano
2. Before quoting another person or repeating an opinion, ask, "Did I understand you right?"
3. Be careful of your statements. Discipline yourself to tell the truth and only the truth. Don't exaggerate it, minimize it, twist it, or mix it with a pinch of anything else.
4. Be careful of your actions. Tell with your face and say with your lips what you are thinking in your mind. If you disagree, don't nod your head. If you are concerned, don't try to act ho-hum. If you are unconcerned, don't make a pretense of being excited.
5. If you have children at home, help them to differentiate between truth and falsehood in the media. Point out, for instance, that the dramatic,

full-scenario, full-sound action toy sequences
in television ads are far different from the plas-
tic junk that is being advertised.

6.. And don't do anything you might be ashamed
to tell the truth about!

Breath Fresheners
Containing a Drop of Truth Syrup

First: You shall not give false testimony against
          your neighbor. (Exod. 20:16)
Second: The LORD hates those who don't keep their
          word, but he delights in those who do.
          (Prov. 12:22 NLT)
Third: Surely you desire truth in the inner parts;
          you teach me wisdom in the inmost place.
          (Ps. 51:6)
Fourth: So put away all falsehood and "tell your
          neighbor the truth" because we belong to
          each other. (Eph. 4:25 NLT)

A Beautiful Tongue Is a Positive Tongue

The people of Israel escaped from the slave camps of Egypt under the leadership of Moses. But it was not until forty years later that they were permitted to enter the Promised Land. Nearly all the people who left Egypt with such high hopes died in the wilderness.

Why were these thousands of people not allowed to enter the "land of milk and honey"? Was it because of idolatry? Sexual immorality? Dishonesty? Violence?

No, it was none of the above. God asked a rhetorical question of Moses and Aaron: "How long will this wicked community grumble against me? I have heard the complaints of these grumbling Israelites" (Num. 14:27).

Then God answered his own question: "In this desert your bodies will fall—every one of you twenty years old or more who was counted in the census and who has grumbled against me. Not one of you will enter the land" (vv. 29–30). The Israelites stumbled because they grumbled.

God had delivered them from tyranny, but their response was to complain about every bump they encountered on the road to freedom. Immobilized by fear and ingratitude, they died in the desert without ever seeing the Promised Land. The sentence for grumbling was death.

"What causes fights and quarrels among you?" asked James. "Don't they come from your desires that battle within you? You want something but don't get it" (James 4:1).

Among those who will be dealt with most harshly at the last judgment, says Jude, are the "grumblers and fault-finders" (Jude 16).

Thorns and Joy

The apostle Paul had plenty to complain about. He had a "thorn in [the] flesh" (2 Cor. 12:7) that must have been painful and inconvenient. He was beaten, shipwrecked, forcibly evicted, and persecuted. He spent two years languishing in a prison without any formal charges being lodged against him. Yet he was no complainer.

> I have learned to be content whatever the circumstances. I know what it is to be in need, and I know what it is to have plenty. I have learned the secret of being content in any and every situation, whether well fed or hungry, whether living in plenty or in want. I can do everything through him who gives me strength. (Phil. 4:11–13)

In this same letter, written from a prison cell, the words

"joy" and "rejoice" appear no less than thirteen times in five short chapters.

"Godliness with contentment," said Paul to Timothy, "is great gain" (1 Tim. 6:6).

"Keep your lives free from the love of money and be content with what you have," said the writer of the letter to the Hebrews, "because God has said, 'Never will I leave you; never will I forsake you'" (Heb. 13:5).

A grumbling and complaining tongue is an ugly tongue.

A contented tongue is a beautiful tongue.

A Positive Tongue Handles Illness with Quiet Strength

We've all met someone who no longer gets asked, "How are you?" The uninitiated soul who unwittingly asks that question is treated to a lengthy and often gory discourse on the most recent operation, the amount of blood lost, and the precise physiological terms for at least half of the organs in the body—to say nothing of last year's arthritis, this year's sinus infection, and a sister's miscarriage.

We've also visited people who were in great pain, yet who maintained a spirit of strong faith and even cheerfulness. Sweat was on the forehead, yet a smile was on the lips. We were inspired and lifted up, and we walked away thinking that our own problems were not so bad after all.

Said Paul, who was no stranger to suffering, to the weakly young Timothy, "Endure hardship with us like a good soldier of Christ Jesus" (2 Tim. 2:3).

It's not easy to speak with a beautiful tongue of peaceful trust when the body is being plagued with pain. It takes more than human power to grin and bear it. It takes the power of God's Holy Spirit. "I can do everything," said Paul, "through him who gives me strength" (Phil. 4:13).

A Positive Tongue Disciplines Itself in the Face of Injustice

It's not easy to keep from complaining. Life isn't always fair. You struggle along honestly, living moderately in order to stay within your income. Meanwhile, the fellow down the street operates a fraudulent business and owns a swimming pool, three cars, a camper, a boat, and four television sets. Your teenage daughter, who is trying to lead a godly and chaste life, gets discouraged because her unprincipled classmates are getting the dates. Your son comes home with honest Cs, and his classmates receive dishonest Bs. It's not always easy to remain positive.

When you're feeling low because of the apparent success of dishonest and immoral people, read Psalm 37. Sometimes called "the psalm for the fretful," it reassures us that God is still a God of justice, and that there is no wrong that will not eventually be made right:

> Don't worry about the wicked.
> Don't envy those who do wrong.
> For like grass, they soon fade away.
> Like springtime flowers, they soon wither.
> (vv. 1–2 NLT)

Are you tempted to complain to God?

> Commit everything you do to the LORD.
> Trust him, and he will help you.
> He will make your innocence as clear as the dawn,
> and the justice of your cause
> will shine like the noonday sun.
> (vv. 5–6 NLT)

Are you tempted to lash out with your tongue in jealous anger?

> Stop your anger!
> Turn from your rage! . . .
> It only leads to harm.
> (v. 8 NLT)

A Positive Tongue Will Improve Your Church Life

In almost every church there are members who are always, always, always complaining about something. On any given Sunday morning, one member will complain that the church is too hot and another will complain that the church is too cold. One will complain that "we always sing the same old hymns" and another will complain that "we always sing unfamiliar hymns," even when, in fact, the congregation has just sung two of each.

Hearing constant complaints is disheartening. It makes ministers less effective and can send spouses on "vacations" to mental institutions. Lay leaders become discouraged when the church people who always have an excuse for not helping are the same ones who sit back and criticize the ones who volunteer. New Christians—who expect to be uplifted and inspired—grow disillusioned when they instead encounter a thistle patch of griping and complaining.

Unfortunately, the people who are the complainers, grumblers, and criticizers often don't recognize themselves. When they read a chapter like this, they point their fingers at someone else. Perhaps you should consider if this chapter is about you.

"Do everything without complaining or arguing," says the Scriptures, "so that you may become blameless and pure, children of God without fault in a crooked and depraved generation, in which you shine like stars in the universe" (Phil. 2:14–15).

A Positive Tongue Will Improve Your Home Life

"Better to live on a corner of the roof than share a house with a quarrelsome wife" (Prov. 25:24). Contentiousness is not, of course, gender-specific. A quarrelsome husband is every bit as aggravating as a quarrelsome wife, and perhaps more dangerous.

While unzipped pants devastate thousands of marriages, unzipped tongues devastate tens of thousands. Nothing is quite so deadly to marital happiness as an endless recitation of a spouse's unfinished projects, personal flaws, choice of ancestors, eating habits, earning ability, and poor personal grooming. The usual responses to these kinds of tongue lashings are to (1) fight back, (2) turn off, or (3) move out.

A similar negativity can pervade the parent/child relationship. One teenager said, "I can do a hundred things right, but all I ever hear about are the few things I do wrong."

And in the opposite vein, don't allow your children to get into the habit of complaining. Require them (yes, you can do that) to display a positive attitude toward school assignments, teachers, chores, and meals.

The way to cure the nag habit is to accentuate the positive. An appreciative tongue (see chap. 3) could have saved the Israelites in the wilderness and can save many a faltering relationship. When you give children, grandchildren, fellow church members, and neighbors an example worthy to be followed, you will "shine like stars in the universe" (Phil. 2:15).

Beauty Exercises
To Transform the Way You Look at Things

1. On a scale of one to ten, rate yourself as a negative or positive speaker, with one being the most negative and ten being the most positive. Now ask members of the family to rate you on the same scale. Compare the two.

2. Think of the things you've criticized concerning your church, school, community, and home. Write these criticisms in one column of a sheet of paper, being as specific as you can. Now, in another column, itemize all you've done in a positive way to correct these faults. After you've done this, vow not to criticize until you've done everything within your power to remedy the situation. In other words, be a builder, not a wrecker.

3. Next time you're ready to complain that there is something you don't have, stop and thank

God for something you do have. Then ask a few questions about whatever you say is lacking. Is it a necessity or a luxury? How much would you actually use it if you had it? Do you want it because you really like it or because someone else has one like it? Could your money be spent more wisely on something else?

4.   Be able to recite the "breath fresheners" that follow. If some are particularly appropriate for you, write them on cards and set them on the cupboard, dresser, or desk.

Breath Fresheners
That Will Make You Nice to Be Near

First: I have learned the secret of being content in any and every situation. (Phil. 4:12)

Second: Godliness with contentment is great gain. (1 Tim. 6:6)

Third: Keep your lives free from the love of money and be content with what you have, because God has said, "Never will I leave you; never will I forsake you." (Heb. 13:5)

Fourth: Do everything without complaining or arguing, so that you may become blameless and pure, children of God without fault in a crooked and depraved generation, in which you shine like stars in the universe. (Phil. 2:14–15)

A Beautiful Tongue Is a Simple Tongue

S *imple* is defined as "without ostentation," "unpretending," "natural," "not ornate," "unembellished." It's the opposite of artificial and pretentious. A beautifully simple tongue is one that makes no effort to impress, to flatter, to embellish, to exaggerate. It does not give the impression that the speaker is richer, wiser, holier, or greater than he or she really is. The words of a simple tongue can be taken at face value. A simple tongue seeks to clarify and illumine.

Jesus Was a Simple Man

Jesus was a simple man. He made no effort to make an impression. He did not choose clothes that drew attention to himself. He did not sensationalize his miracles. He made no effort to be seen socializing with the "right" people.

Jesus spoke in simple words. He told parables and drew analogies from the common things of life, like mustard seeds and sheepfolds. He didn't try to tone down his more pointed remarks. He didn't use obscure words or intellectual-sounding phrases. As a result, the crowds heard him "with delight" (Mark 12:37).

The Words of the Gospel Message Are Simple Words

The apostle Paul believed he should follow the example of his Master regarding simplicity of speech. He came preaching, he said, "not with words of human wisdom, lest the cross of Christ be emptied of its power" (1 Cor. 1:17). Then he added that the simple, unembellished truth of God is far more effective in saving the world than all the fancy wisdom of the age:

> But God chose the foolish things of the world to shame the wise; God chose the weak things of the world to shame the strong. He chose the lowly things of this world and the despised things—and the things that are not—to nullify the things that are, so that no one may boast before him. (1 Cor. 1:27–29)

The simple, heartfelt, even faltering testimony of a person whose life has been changed is more effective in winning a person to Christ than the erudite lecture of a theologian.

A Simple Tongue Uses a "Yes" or "No"

Jesus said, "But I tell you, Do not swear at all; either by heaven . . . or by the earth . . . or by Jerusalem . . . [or] by your head. . . . Simply let your 'Yes' be 'Yes,' and your 'No,' 'No'; anything beyond this comes from the evil one" (Matt. 5:34–37).

Swearing does not refer to profanity. It refers to the making of oaths in order to convince somebody you are telling the truth. But others should be able to assume that we are telling the truth without some kind of verbal reinforcement. We shouldn't have to "swear on a stack of Bibles" or say "hell no" or "for heaven's sake yes."

A Simple Tongue Doesn't Try to Impress Others

"Love . . . does not boast," says 1 Corinthians 13:4; or as Phillips translates it, "Love . . . is neither anxious to impress nor does it cherish inflated ideas of its own importance."

People with a simple tongue resist the temptation to announce how much they lose when the stock market goes down a hundred points; or to "witness" about how many hours they spend in prayer; or to tell about how they have increased their tithe to 12 percent; or to describe in infinite detail their last three cruises; or to talk with authority about books they haven't actually read; or to talk endlessly about how smart/rich/cute their children/grandchildren/great-grandchildren are; or to quote an "authority" that no one else has heard. A beautiful tongue is a humble tongue.

The more we try to impress others, the less we impress others. Our off-handed, thinly disguised boasts don't fool anyone and often produce an effect opposite from what we intended. People who are genuinely great don't have to ballyhoo their accomplishments. Accomplishments speak for themselves.

The bottom line is this: Our real emphasis should be on *being,* not on *seeming to be.*

A Simple Tongue Avoids Flattery

Gushers are welcome only on oil fields. And even there they are quickly capped.

Many of our compliments are meant to impress other people rather than to express our impression of them. Many of our compliments are designed to make others feel good about us rather than to make them feel good about themselves. When a compliment disguises ulterior motives, it's called flattery, and flattery is a form of lie. When you appreciate something, say it (see chap. 3), but say it simply, briefly, and sincerely.

A Simple Tongue Avoids Exaggeration

"If I've told you once, I've told you a million times—don't exaggerate!"

Titus 2:7 says that in our teaching we are to "show integrity, seriousness and soundness of speech."

If the incident you are relating is funny, there is no need to make it funnier by embellishing. If the fish you caught was eleven and a half inches long, say it was eleven and a half inches long. If you had surgery, there is no need to make it sound worse than it was (if, indeed, you need to describe it at all). If your children are intelligent, that fact should be obvious to all, and you won't have to conjure up a story about how their teachers praise them. If you are in a certain economic bracket, what good will it do to give the impression that you are more affluent?

A Simple Tongue Sets Us Free

Those who have learned the discipline of simplicity are truly free—free to be themselves, free from the burden of always being "on stage," free from the oppression of others' opinions, free from the worry of making the right impression, free from the concern of getting credit—in short, free from the tyranny of their own ego.

A Simple Tongue Uses Simple Language with God

"Holy and infinite Jehovah, we beseech thee," drones the minister, "look down upon us, Thy humble servants, in Thine infinite mercy and with Thine ineffable love . . ."

That's the kind of pastoral prayer that many of us grew up with. There is a certain dignity and beauty about such language, but are dignity and beauty the objectives of prayer? Does the use of high-sounding words increase the effectiveness of the prayer? Do they encourage others to lead in public prayer? Who are we trying to impress—people or God? Is prayer intended to make an impression?

Jesus advocated simplicity in prayer. He said, "And when you pray, do not keep on babbling like pagans, for they think they will be heard because of their many words"

(Matt. 6:7). Then he taught his followers a model prayer that is the epitome of directness and simplicity. There is no fluff, no fancy language in the Lord's Prayer—just simple praise and direct petition.

The publican's prayer, which effectively asked for forgiveness, was only seven words long (Luke 18:13). Paul prayed for the removal of the thorn in his flesh, not a hundred times or even ten times, but only three times (2 Cor. 12:8).

The best way to pray is naturally, normally, simply, and sincerely.

Beauty Exercises
To Eliminate Unnecessary Flab

1. Lead a prayer in Bible study, in Sunday school, or in some other setting without using flowery language or impressive phrases.
2. Relate a humorous incident that happened to you last week without exaggerating even one small detail.
3. Make a list of the things you have purchased and then seldom or never used. Why did you buy them? Was it because you thought they would be valuable additions to your life? Did you buy them because someone else had similar things, and you wanted to keep up? Did you buy them so you could talk about them?
4. Suppress the temptation to use a newly learned big word to impress your guests.

5. Give a compliment to someone from whom you have nothing to gain.
6. Evaluate your prayer life. Are you using a lot of fancy words? Are you repeating the same things over and over again without thinking? Are you badgering God about things for which he's given you an answer long ago?

Breath Fresheners
That Will Help Keep the Words You Breathe Pure

First: Simply let your "Yes" be "Yes," and your "No," "No"; anything beyond this comes from the evil one. (Matt. 5:37)

Second: And when you pray, do not keep on babbling like pagans, for they think they will be heard because of their many words. (Matt. 6:7)

Third: Love . . . is not possessive: it is neither anxious to impress nor does it cherish inflated ideas of its own importance. (1 Cor. 13:4 PHILLIPS)

Fourth: God chose the foolish things of the world to shame the wise; God chose the weak things of the world to shame the strong. (1 Cor. 1:27)

Leader's Guide

Introduction to This Guide

In this brief space it is not possible to tell you how to become a good group leader for your Bible study. Much has been written on how to become a better teacher, how to lead a discussion, how to be a leader of small groups, and how to develop other leadership skills. Make use of all possible aids to prepare yourself in a general way for the task of leading a Bible study. Attend seminars, participate in leadership conventions, read books, and—most importantly—learn from experience.

This Study Guide Is Not Predigested

This is not a predigested study guide. In other words, the guide will not tell you, step by step, how to present each lesson. It will give you some help, but by-and-large you're on your own.

Some leaders will teach by lecturing. Some will do it primarily by discussion. Some will wish to role-play. The best method is a variety of methods. No matter what you do, it can get tiresome if it's the same all the time.

What This Guide Contains

This leader's guide is not meant to be comprehensive. We hope you will go to other sources for additional material. We have included, however, a number of items that will be helpful in leading a group study of the "beauty care" material. You will find

1. suggestions on how to introduce, present, or enhance the topic. Lesson 1, for instance, contains a "quickie poll" that can be used to generate interest in the topic and give the leader helpful information.
2. discussion questions. You will, no doubt, think of others, but these will give you a start. You can use some for discussion by the entire group and others for small-group discussions and reports.
3. illustrations and additional material, so you can supplement the main text.
4. additional Scripture references to supplement those used in the lesson and the "breath fresheners."
5. exercises, research projects, and other things to do as a class.

Additional Resource Materials

Do not be content with what has been given to you in this guide. Consult resource books for additional material. Browse in your church and public libraries. Talk about the subject with a spouse or a friend. Don't be afraid to ask for help from your pastor, who may have helpful materials in the files as well as useful books in a personal library. Sources include Bible commentaries, Bible dictionaries, books of illustrations, books of quotations, and practical/inspirational self-help books.

Also—and this is very important—keep your eyes and ears open for current materials that illustrate the subject. This means previewing all the lessons beforehand so you know what to look for. Check newspaper stories, magazine articles, and novels; listen to comments made by friends and neighbors; use personal incidents from your own life.

Using the "Beauty Exercises"

Each lesson contains a number of "beauty exercises" —practical suggestions on how the participants can put into practice the principles suggested in the study. These exercises can provide a wealth of material for discussion. Ask a class member, for instance, if he or she has tried beauty exercise number three and how well he or she did with it.

Using the "Breath Fresheners"

Each lesson also includes four "breath fresheners"— four Bible verses to commit to memory. Memorization is valuable because in the process of learning and repeating, the meaning can become deeply immersed in the soul.

You can encourage the memorization of these verses by (1) suggesting that each participant memorize a new verse each week (or every other day if you meet weekly) and at the same time review all the previous verses, (2) demonstrating to them how you have written verses on cards to carry with you for frequent reference, and (3) having the group repeat the verses in unison at each class session. Perhaps this can be done as a concluding act of worship with everyone standing.

Emphasizing the Positive

One final note. You will notice that every chapter title in this study guide emphasizes the positive: "A Beautiful Tongue Is . . ." This positive emphasis is deliberate. It's easy for a study of this kind to degenerate into a litany of ugliness and condemnation. It is important for the class to seek the good rather than to wring its hands over evil; to explore the wonderful possibilities of speech rather than to deplore its sad results; to emphasize virtues rather than sins. And, of course, the class leader sets the tone!

The Importance of a Beautiful Tongue

Stir interest in the subject and gain pertinent information by taking a quickie poll of the group. Distribute copies of the questionnaire below, asking participants to fill them out early in the meeting (unsigned, of course), and then have a helper compile the results for you while the meeting is in progress. Report the results to the group as part of your lesson presentation (a chalkboard may help). You may wish to use the questions and the compiled statistics as a springboard for discussion.

1. I have trouble controlling my tongue (a) never, (b) seldom, (c) sometimes, (d) frequently.
2. After having a difference of opinion with someone, I usually feel that I was most hurt by (a) the issues involved, or (b) the words said.

3. As for indulging in gossip, I feel that I am (a) never guilty, (b) seldom guilty, (c) sometimes guilty, (d) frequently guilty of it.

4. During this past week I was able to use my tongue constructively by
   _____ comforting a child
   _____ expressing love to a spouse or special friend
   _____ advising a friend
   _____ encouraging a fellow worker
   _____ witnessing for Christ
   _____ defending a good cause
   _____ expressing sympathy and concern
   _____ teaching a lesson or skill
   _____ other_____

5. Generally, I believe I talk (a) too much, (b) too little, (c) about the right amount.

6. Check the faulty uses of the tongue that bother you most in other people (mark three):*
   _____ talking too much
   _____ being unappreciative
   _____ never witnessing
   _____ using profanity
   _____ complaining
   _____ being unkind
   _____ spreading gossip
   _____ lying
   _____ exaggerating

*Note: these nine choices are the negative side of the nine topics covered in the book.

Use a Mirror to Introduce the Subject

Bring to class a hand mirror—preferably the kind that magnifies. Walk around the class, stop in front of various people, ask them to stick out their tongue and look at it in the mirror. Ask them a question about what they see. This should trigger a few chuckles while focusing the consciousness of the class on the tongue. Questions could include

- Has anyone ever whistled at your tongue?
- Can you catch flies with your tongue? (Some frogs can!)
- Have you ever gone shopping for your tongue?
- Have you ever dieted for your tongue?
- Have you ever followed an exercise regimen for your tongue?
- Can you smell with your tongue? (Snakes and some lizards can!)
- Have you ever had your tongue photographed by a professional photographer?
- Can you chew with your tongue? (Some fish can!)

Tell the class that although everyone answered "no" to these questions, their tongue is one of the most important parts of their body.

Use a Chalkboard or Dry-Erase Board to Focus on the Subject

Draw a vertical line down the middle of the chalkboard, creating two columns. At the top of one column write, "An ugly tongue is a tongue that . . ." and at the top of the other column write, "A beautiful tongue is a tongue that . . ."

Ask class members to complete the sentences as specifically as possible. You may get answers like "doesn't betray a confidence," "says 'I love you,'" "says, 'You did a good job,'" "doesn't yell at other drivers."

Participants may suggest more answers for the "ugly" column than for the "beautiful" column, so try to keep the two columns balanced.

You may wish to write down these class contributions for future use, since it is likely that most of them will fit into the remaining nine lessons of this book.

Discuss James 3:5–8

"Consider what a great forest is set on fire by a small spark," said James (3:5b). What kind of fires can the tongue ignite? Possibilities: fires at home, work, school, church, highway, and so on.

"It is a restless evil, full of deadly poison," said James (3:8). Which relationships are the tongue most likely to poison? Possibilities: husband/wife, parent/child, mother-in-law/daughter-in-law, pastor/congregation, and so on.

Conduct a Testimony (and Confession) Time

How did you use your gift of speech constructively during the past week? During the past month? During the past year?

What was your most embarrassing situation involving something you said?

Add Additional Material: The Human Tongue Is Distinctive

Some animals have fancier tongues than humans have. Snakes and lizards have forked tongues that also serve as organs of smell. Teeth grow on the tongues of salmon and trout. Some frogs, toads, and chameleons have long tongues that can dart out with blinding speed to capture insects.

Although our human tongues cannot harpoon a dinner, bite, or smell, they can do something even more fantastic —they can form words. The gift of speech makes us distinctive from the animal world and gives us a tremendous potential for both good and evil.

Look Ahead to the Next Lesson

It's important for the class leader to look ahead to the next lesson. Alert your class to the subject, "A Beautiful Tongue Is a Silent Tongue," and make assignments and suggestions as necessary. Stress the importance of Scripture memorization, and challenge participants to learn the "Breath Fresheners."

Close by Praying for This Study

Pray for yourself as the leader, for every member of the class, and for the Holy Spirit to control every tongue.

A Beautiful Tongue Is a Silent Tongue

Remind the class of the importance of memorizing each lesson's "Breath Fresheners." Recite the verses together or ask for volunteers to share a verse they have memorized.

Consider the Benefits of Silence

As each is introduced, list the five benefits of constructive silence on a chalkboard. Ask the group members to suggest additional benefits and add them to the list. Have some ideas of your own and be ready to contribute them.

Discuss Silence in the Family Setting

Discuss how practical the following rule might be for your families: "If you can't say anything nice about a person, don't say it." (Some families have established this as a mealtime rule.) What are its advantages? Disadvantages? How important is the parents' example?

Do you think that husbands and wives really listen to each other? Why or why not? Do they listen to each other less as time goes on?

Do you agree that many extramarital affairs begin innocently, with one person needing to talk and another person willing to listen? Should this potential danger eliminate cross-gender friendships? How can husbands and wives guard against these situations getting out of hand?

Discuss Constructive and Destructive Silence

In what kinds of situations is it best to keep silent, not saying anything at all? Be specific.

We have spoken in this lesson about "constructive silence," implying that there may be other kinds. Can silence be used destructively as well as constructively? Which is worse, the noisy argument or the silent treatment?

Musicians have said that music consists of two elements: sound and silence. What do you suppose they mean by that? Could the same be said of other kinds of communication?

Discuss God's Revelation in Silence

What do you suppose 1 Kings 19:11–12a means when it says "the LORD was not in the wind . . . in the earthquake . . . in the fire"? Doesn't God reveal himself in nature, even in loud and destructive natural events?

Does God still communicate in "a gentle whisper" (v. 12b)? What does this mean? Has God ever communicated with you in this way? What may be required in order to hear the "gentle whispers" of God? (Perhaps turn down the television, set aside some quiet time, take a walk in nature, "tune in to God," and so on.)

Ask for Personal Illustrations

Encourage class members to relate an amusing (at least in retrospect) incident in which they embarrassed themselves by talking too much or saying the wrong thing. Relating a story from your own experience will encourage class members to participate. Your example will prime the pump, so to speak, and assure the class that it's okay to make themselves vulnerable.

Challenge Class Members to Develop "A Personal Program for Constructive Silence"

Divide the class into small groups of three or four people. Ask each group to generate four or five suggestions for a "Personal Program of Constructive Silence." Ask each group to write their ideas on newsprint and/or report them to the larger group. Compare, contrast, and summarize, using these suggestions as the basis for a master list.

Suggest How Class Members Can Be Good Listeners

Here are some suggestions for becoming an effective sounding board:

1. Always keep a confidence. Never spread to someone else a tidbit that has been told to you

in confidence, even though you introduce it
with, "Don't pass this on to anyone else."

2. Don't feel compelled to express agreement or
   disagreement with every statement made.

3. Refrain from minimizing others' problems by
   relating your own.

4. Be slow to give advice. Your friend, by talking
   it through with you, will probably come to his
   or her own decision—which is the only one that
   matters.

5. To help the other person understand herself or
   himself, ask questions such as "Why do you
   feel that way?" and "You've changed your opinion about that, haven't you?"

6. Keep the conversation going by repeating the
   last thing the other person said: "Then you
   really feel you can stand up to your boss on
   that issue?"

7. Always keep a confidence. (Yes, I know we've
   said it before.)

Prepare the Class for the Next Topic

Prepare for the next lesson, "A Beautiful Tongue Is
an Appreciative Tongue," by asking class members to
be especially appreciative of others between now and
the next class.

Close with Silent Prayer

Close with a period of *silent* prayer, so no one feels
an obligation to speak. Suggest that class members listen
to God as well as speaking to him during this time.

A Beautiful Tongue Is an Appreciative Tongue

Ask members of the group to share the Scripture verses they have memorized. Be sure to respond to each contribution with a genuine and enthusiastic expression of thanks.

Share Additional Scripture References to an Appreciative Tongue

Nor should there be obscenity, foolish talk or coarse joking, which are out of place, but rather thanksgiving. (Eph. 5:4)

And whatever you do, whether in word or deed, do it all in the name of the Lord

Jesus, giving thanks to God the Father through him. (Col. 3:17)

Then he took the cup, gave thanks and offered it to them, and they all drank from it. (Mark 14:23)

Consider the Dire Results of an Unappreciative Tongue

Paul, in Romans 1, says that when people fail to honor and thank God, their lives degenerate into idolatry and immorality. We don't ordinarily make this connection, do we? Why do you suppose thanklessness triggers other sins? Why does a lack of appreciation have such a devastating effect on the human soul?

Give the Lepers an Excuse for Thanklessness

Review the story of Jesus and the ten lepers as recorded in Luke 17:11–19. If you could ask each of the nine cured lepers why they failed to thank Jesus, what do you suppose they would say? Using the board or newsprint to record the answers, ask the class to invent an excuse for each of the nine. Here are some possibilities: "I had to go to my doctor to confirm that I was really healed." "I came back later, but Jesus was no longer there." "My first priority was to go to my family and share the good news." "I fully intend to send Jesus a thank-you card, but I just haven't gotten around to it."

Discuss the Miracles of an Appreciative Tongue

When we feel appreciative, we sometimes fail to express it. Ask class members to share situations that can serve as examples. Perhaps a stranger helped with a tire one wintry night, or friends sent flowers and made personal calls at the hospital, or the pastor gave an exceptionally fine sermon, or a teacher twenty years ago sparked an interest in math or music—and received no appreciative response. Be prepared to get things rolling by sharing a confession or two of your own.

Our last lesson on the beauty of a silent tongue suggested that the person who really listens to a spouse takes a proactive step in strengthening the solidarity of the relationship. The same can be said of a husband or wife who regularly and sincerely expresses appreciation to his or her spouse. Ask the class, When was the last time you complimented your husband or wife? When your mate goes out of the way to do something nice, do you acknowledge it? Love thrives on praise.

We may expect our children to appreciate what we do for them. Would it also help if we as parents regularly expressed our appreciation to our children for what they mean to us?

Do an Exercise in Appreciation

Ask each person in the class, right here and now, to turn to the person in the next seat and express what he or she appreciates about that person. There are several ways you can do this. One way is to ask the person sitting at one end of each row to say something nice to the next person. Then that person will compliment the next one, and so on. When the words of appreciation reach the end of the row, send them back to where they started.

Give an Appreciation Assignment

This assignment is very important. Challenge every class member to implement the first "Beauty Exercise" in the study book: Consciously express appreciation to at least five people before the next class session, noting their responses. Tell class members that they will have an opportunity to share their experiences at the next class session.

Close with Prayers of Appreciation

For closing prayers, ask class members to follow the instructions of Philippians 4:6 and accompany each petition or request with a statement of thanksgiving.

A Beautiful Tongue Is a Witnessing Tongue

If you are studying this lesson during December, you can tie it in with the Christmas story by referring the class to Luke 2:17–18: "When they had seen him, they spread the word concerning what had been told them about this child, and all who heard it were amazed at what the shepherds said to them."

The shepherds immediately became witnesses to others. They were so overwhelmed by the good news they had received and experienced that they couldn't refrain from telling everybody. They didn't wait until they knew all the facts and understood all the theological implications; they didn't wait until they had been trained by experts; they didn't care whether or not people called them fanatics. They just told it as they had seen it—personally, forcefully, thankfully, and immediately.

Study the Story About the Man Who Was Delivered of Demons

Refer to the story of the man whose demons were cast by Jesus into a herd of pigs (Mark 5:1–20). When the healed man volunteered to go with Jesus—presumably to go into full-time service—Jesus turned him down and told him to be a witness in his own neighborhood (v. 19). Why do you suppose Jesus responded in the way he did? Why could this man's testimony be effective? Why are lay people sometimes more effective witnesses than clergy? Is there a lesson here for us? Can our testimony be effective, even if it isn't as dramatic as this man's story?

Evaluate the Importance of Being a "Christian Presence"

In small groups or in class as a whole, evaluate the effectiveness of being a "Christian presence"—that is, displaying Christian character but not necessarily adding a verbal witness. Is being a Christian enough? Should we say we are Christians? There's a gospel song that says, "They will know we are Christian by our love." What do these words assume? (Hint: the song assumes that [1] we as Christians will, in fact, be distinctive by the love we demonstrate, and [2] others will know that our love is based on Christian convictions.)

Discuss What's Effective and What's Not

If you watch football on television, you've seen hand-printed "John 3:16" signs in the end zone. Is this kind of witness effective? Do you think nonbelievers look up

John 3:16 to see what it says? Do you think displays like this give a positive impression of the Christian faith?

Evaluate the effectiveness of such "witnessing tools" as Christian bumper stickers, Scripture screen savers, Christian slogans on sweatshirts, W.W.J.D. ("What would Jesus do?") bracelets, and so on. Discuss the positive and negative effect of each.

Discuss the effectiveness of preaching on a street corner, talking to strangers on the beach, witnessing door-to-door, and placing tracts on windshields. What are the negatives of these techniques? The positives?

Rate the Effectiveness of Life Stories

What kind of life stories are appropriate to share with others as Christian testimonies? Can you relate some examples of appropriate stories? What kind of stories, if any, are inappropriate or of limited value?

In addition to sharing a story from your life, what other words or acts can be valuable as a Christian witness? (Hint: they need not be major productions. Sometimes off-hand, seemingly unimportant remarks and actions can be valuable, such as saying "As we were getting ready for church last Sunday . . ." or "This is what Mary made in Sunday school last week," or "I bet your kids would enjoy vacation Bible school.")

Review Scripture Passages

There is an advantage to memorizing (or knowing where to find) key Scripture verses to use when sharing your testimony. Here are some of the important verses:

- God's love for us—John 3:16; 10:10
- Our need to get right with God—Romans 3:23; 6:23
- What Christ has done for us—John 14:6; 1 Timothy 2:5; 1 Peter 3:18
- The necessary steps of repentance and faith— John 1:12; Ephesians 2:8–9; 1 John 1:9

Role-Play a Verbal Witness

Ask a couple of talented class members to demonstrate examples of effective and ineffective Christian testimonies. Ask the class to discuss what went right and what went wrong, then to make suggestions for improvement. Possible scenarios: a wedding guest tells strangers across the table how God helped him with an alcohol problem; neighbors discuss the pros and cons of church-going; a passer-by comforts a motorcyclist injured in an accident; a person is invited by a coworker to go golfing on Sunday morning.

Share Faith Stories with Each Other

Divide the class into groups of three or four. Ask the group members to share with each other short testimonies of what God has done in their lives and the "reason for their hope." It's important not just to *talk about* witnessing. We have to actually do it, and a good place to start is with fellow believers.

Pray for Guidance in Witnessing

Close by praying (1) for ourselves, that we may overcome our fear of speaking up about our faith, and (2) for others, that God will prepare them to be receptive to our witness.

A Beautiful Tongue Is a Clean Tongue

The best way to encourage class members to keep memorizing the "breath fresheners" is to highlight them in class. You can help the class commit the verses to memory by reading them together in unison a few times, then putting down the books and repeating them from memory. With today's short verses, this should be easy.

Illustrate the Holiness of God's Name

You may wish to use the following illustration to emphasize the holiness of the name of God:

Sometimes when an outstanding athlete retires from a college or professional sports career, that player's number is "retired" too. If his or her suit number is 33, no one will ever use the number 33 on that team in the future. The number is set apart for that person alone as a token of esteem and honor. No other athlete will ever share its glory.

Similarly, the name of God has been "retired." No one else can use it. The name is for his exclusive use. It is a holy (literally "set apart") name, to be treated with reverence and honor. "I am the Lord; that is my name!" says one of our breath fresheners, "I will not give my glory to another" (Isa. 42:8).

Discuss What Constitutes Profanity

Does the scope of the third commandment include the various names for Jesus and the Holy Spirit as well as the names of God the Father? Why?

What about the slang words that are a little different from the holy names but sound very much like them?

Discuss Profanity as "Inferior Communication"

The study book says that "If the use of trite language identifies an amateur writer, profanity identifies an amateur talker. . . . Even if profanity were spiritually and ethically acceptable, it would be an inferior form of communication." Is this statement too harsh? Why or why not?

Discuss the Proper Response to People Who Swear

Discuss the best way to handle a social situation in which people around you are cursing and swearing—perhaps at a bowling alley, golf course, office, dinner party, cafeteria, assembly line, or wherever. Is it helpful to ask people to stop swearing? Is it helpful to say something like "You're talking about a friend of mine, and I prefer that you wouldn't use his name like that"? Or is it better just to ignore it and keep your own speech clean?

Conduct a Class Research Project

Appoint a committee (of willing participants) to do a study of offensive language on television. Is there an increase of profanity on television programs? Why do you think this is true? Who regulates language on television? What rules are in place? Are these rules being followed? Which television programs consistently use the most offensive language? In what way is this language offensive?

Do you think there ought to be more limitations on the language used in the media? Who decides on limitations? What are the dangers of censorship? What are the alternatives to censorship?

Ask the committee to assemble a list of the names and addresses of companies that advertise on programs that feature profanity with reckless abandon. Organize a letter-writing campaign that advocates clean speech.

Discuss Swearing as a "Habit"

"It's only a habit." What does the class think about this common excuse for swearing? Are we responsible for habits? How do habits originate? Are there good habits and bad habits? Are good deeds less praiseworthy because they are repeated often and have become habitual? Are bad deeds less blameworthy because they are repeated often enough to become habitual?

Look Ahead to the Next Chapter

Alert the class to chapter six, "A Beautiful Tongue Is a Kind Tongue." You may wish to assign "Beauty Exercise" 6, which is to write an original paraphrase of 1 Corinthians 13:1–3.

Close with Prayer

Ask God to cleanse and control the tongue. Even more importantly, ask God to cleanse and control the mind, which tells the tongue what to say.

A Beautiful Tongue Is a Kind Tongue

A gentle answer turns away wrath," says Proverbs 15:1, "but a harsh word stirs up anger."

What do you think a "gentle" answer is?

A gentle answer is a quiet answer. An old man once advised young newlyweds, "Never raise your voices unless the house is on fire."

A gentle answer is also a nonargumentative answer. It may defend, but it doesn't lash back. It may stand stoutly for the truth, but it doesn't criticize.

A gentle answer is not a weak answer or a powerless answer. It is, in fact, the strongest kind of answer, because it has the capability of subduing one of humankind's most vicious weapons—an angry tongue.

Add Thoughts to "A Kind Tongue Is a Positive Witness"

Colossians 4:6 says that our speech is to be "seasoned with salt." What do you suppose that means? Salt has two uses: it preserves things, and it makes things more palatable. It doesn't really change food, but it makes it more pleasant to the taste. It makes the difference between just eating food and enjoying food. Likewise, graciousness does not necessarily change the contents of the message we bring, but it does make it more acceptable, pleasant, and believable.

Discuss How a Loving Tongue Keeps All the Commandments

How does a kind and loving tongue relate to the first commandment? The second? The seventh? The tenth? (And all of them in between.)

Discuss Where It Is Most Difficult to Be Kind

Where do you find it most difficult to be kind? At home? At church? At work? In traffic? Why? Under what circumstances are we most likely to be unkind?

Discuss Madalyn Murray O'Hair

Do you think the author is correct when he says that "All too often, Christians fail to accompany their moral convictions with a touch of kindness"? Do you think, for instance, that Madalyn Murray O'Hair was deeply impressed by the kindness of Christians who disagreed with her? Do you think that some Christians are being sufficiently kind to those who have differing opinions on such issues as homosexuality, prayer in public schools, abortion, and assisted suicide?

Discuss Whether the Tongue Can Be Trained to Be Kind

Do you think we can train our tongues to become more kind? Can we become more kind by trying harder? If so, how can we go about doing this? (Accept several suggestions and write them on the board or newsprint.)

Discuss the Difference Between Kindness and Diplomacy

What is the difference between being kind and being diplomatic? How are kindness and diplomacy related? Can kindness be used to manipulate?

Share Occasions of Kindness

Ask class members to share an incident in which someone said a kind word to them, then ask them to tell why the kindness was significant at that time. (It may have resulted in a change of lifestyle, or it may have helped them to overcome discouragement, or it may have merely provided a warm feeling, but in any case it was important.)

Write a Paraphrase of 1 Corinthians 13:1–3

In class do "Beauty Exercise" 6 of the study book section. Give class members five minutes to write a paraphrase of 1 Corinthians 13:1–3 and especially verse 3, as it relates to their vocation, home life, recreation, church life, or whatever. A mother's version, for instance, might be "If I give my children all the toys they could ask for, and if I deliver my automobile for my teenager to use every night, but if I don't take time for them, I have nothing." A church member's version might be, "If I make a generous pledge to the church, and if I attend every meeting, but if I am critical of fellow members on the way home after church, I have nothing." Ask class members to share what they have written.

Close with a Prayer for Kindness

In your closing prayer, confess that there have been times when kindness seemed to evaporate in a cloud of frustration, stress, and anger. Pray for the grace of a kind and forgiving spirit.

A Beautiful Tongue Is a Nongossiping Tongue

Suggest that your study group begin a "Gossip Book." (Present this seriously, tongue-in-cheek of course, and see what kind of comments you get.) Tell members of the group that you will provide a notebook with blank pages. If they have a criticism or complaint against someone or have heard a story about someone, they should write it in this book and sign it. You will then bring the book to the person written about, ask her or him to read it, and request a written reply on the same page.

Discuss the Harmful Effects of Gossip

Divide into small groups and ask each group to think of as many harmful effects of gossip as they can. Set a time limit and ask each group to appoint a reporter. After the entire group is together again, ask one person to report for each group and record the ideas on a board. Responses might include that gossip is (1) a negative witness for Christ, (2) harmful to the reputation of others, (3) a bad example for children, (4) an offense against love, and that it (5) cannot be retrieved, (6) can destroy the reputations of innocent people, (7) has few, if any, positive results.

What Others Have Said

> Gossip is like mud thrown against a clean wall; it may not stick, but it leaves a mark. (source unknown)

> The difference between gossip and news is whether you hear it or tell it. (source unknown)

> A dog is loved by old and young; he wags his tail and not his tongue. (source unknown)

> Everybody says it, and what everybody says must be true. (James Fenimore Cooper)

Play "Guess What They'll Say Next"

Announce that you are going to conduct a quiz. You will give some commonly heard statements ending with the word "but," and the participants must supply the last part of the sentence.

1. "I'm not one to gossip, but_____."
2. "I'm not a bigot, and some of them are my best friends, but _____."
3. "I don't mean to imply that Jean isn't doing a good job as committee chairperson, but _____."
4. "The Reverend is a fine minister in many ways, but _____."

Begin a "Gossip Hot Line"

Give the person on the end of each row a piece of paper on which you have typed a detailed account of an "incident" that people are likely to gossip about. Have each end person read the paper carefully, fold it over, then whisper its contents to the next person, who in turn whispers it to the next person. When the message has reached the end of each row, ask each person on the end to relate the story as he or she heard it, then ask each person at the beginning of the row to read the story from the piece of paper.

You may wish to write your gossip stories along this line:

> Did you know that Patricia and Taylor Schmiddle sold their home for $113,000 and have spent a week visiting their son Tim and his family in Naperville, Illinois? Patricia said that Taylor has been having trouble with his boss at the hardware store, and that their daughter, Ann, who is only fifteen, might be pregnant.

Close with Prayer

Ask God for help as you examine yourselves in the matter of gossip and as you discipline your speech according to the high standard of Philippians 4:8.

A Beautiful Tongue Is a Truthful Tongue

In preparation for the class, ask members to jot down situations during the week in which they were personally tempted to be less than truthful.

Discuss Euphemisms for Lies

Lies often go by more politically sensitive names. President Nixon, you may recall, admitted to giving "inoperative statements" about his involvement in Watergate, and President Clinton never did use the *L* word in his admissions to the American people. Public figures often speak of "misstatements" and "errors." Even the words used to describe lies are often, in fact, lies. Can you think of other terms that are used to soften that harsh word *lie?* How effective are these terms in hiding or softening the reality?

Discuss Teaching Children to Tell the Truth

How do parents distinguish between a child's innocent world of fantasy and a child's attempt to deceive?
Discuss common excuses ("I can't go to school because
my stomach hurts"), buck-passing ("Billy hit me first"),
and outright deception ("Don't worry, Mom; Amy's parents will be home"). Discuss techniques for teaching children always to tell the truth. (These could include calling
immediate attention to untruths, not allowing excuses,
probing all questionable statements, and, of course, consistently showing a good example.)

Discuss the Dynamics of Self-Deception

Some people apparently lie, not to deceive others, but
to deceive themselves. By altering or ignoring the facts,
they create a reality they can live with. Is this necessarily
bad? How can it be beneficial? Harmful?

View Excerpts from Liar, Liar

Play a scene or two from the movie *Liar, Liar* (it's
available at video stores). This movie posits a lawyer who
is unable to lie. Although the video contains some questionable scenes (especially a brief office affair), it also
makes a humorous but convincing case for telling the truth.
Fletcher Reed, an attorney played by Jim Carrey, constantly resorts to falsehoods in his personal and professional life. When Fletcher lies to his son, Max, once again
failing to show up at his birthday party and giving a lame
excuse, Max makes a wish that "for one day Dad can't

tell a lie." Max's wish comes true, and Fletcher's life is thrown into total and hilarious disarray. But in the end he discovers that, as he says, "the truth will make you free."

Discuss the Dynamics of "White Lies"

Ask the group to suggest additional situations in which a person might have good reasons for not telling the truth. This could be a role play in which small groups devise and act out situations, which the whole group could then discuss. When is falsehood justified? What principles apply? What can be the short-term results? The long-term results? Can white lies become habitual?

Analyze Some Common Excuses

Suggest how the following statements are probably not the full truth and write a statement that is more likely the whole truth:

- "The kids in the back seat distracted me" (I wasn't paying full attention to my driving).
- "It's an old football injury" (I'm slowing down).
- "Harry hit me first" (Because I called him a wimp).
- "The clerk must have given me the wrong size" (I've gained weight).
- "I've got a headache" (I'm not in the mood).
- "A sudden breeze caught the ball" (I've got to improve my swing).
- "The check's in the mail" (It will be soon).
- "We had a computer problem" (I entered the wrong data).

- "I left my job because of something the boss said" ("You're fired").
- "I can't remember" (Unfortunately, I can).
- "I gave at the office" (I have no desire to give— period).
- "I'll do it in a minute" (Or whenever I feel like it).

Discuss "Evangelist's Estimate"

An "evangelist's estimate" is common parlance for a highly exaggerated claim of attendance at a rally or public gathering. Typically, the police estimate of attendance at a rally in Washington, D.C., is about half that of the organizer's estimate. How do you suppose the higher figure became known as an "evangelist's estimate"? Is this a form of lying? Would Christian people lie about something like this?

Close with Prayer

Pray that God will help everyone in the group have a finely tuned sense of right and wrong, truth and untruth. Pray that all of us may so live that we have no reason to lie.

A Beautiful Tongue Is a Positive Tongue

Some may wonder whether God was being a bit harsh with the people of Israel about their grumbling. To show the extent of Israel's negativism, ask various class members to look up and read in class a number of short passages: Exodus 14:10–12; 15:22–24; 16:2–3, 6–8; 17:1–2, 7; Numbers 11:1; 12:1–2; 14:1–3.

Illustrate the Point with Hummingbirds and Vultures

Tell about a hummingbird and a vulture who were flying over the same territory. The hummingbird found a flower and the vulture found a rotting carcass. The point is this: We find what we look for. If we look for the negative, we will surely find it. If we concentrate on the positive, we will find that.

Illustrate Negative and Positive with a Glass of Water

Fill a large glass exactly half full with colored liquid, such as a soft drink. Ask, Is the glass half full or is it half empty? Both are true, of course, so what difference does it make how you describe it?

Discuss Contentment and Stoicism

About 300 B.C. the Greek philosopher Zeno taught that people should be free from passion and should calmly accept everything that happens as the unavoidable result of the divine will. This philosophy came to be known as stoicism. Today a stoic is usually defined as a person who is seemingly indifferent to or unaffected by joy, grief, pleasure, or pain.

There's a well-known prayer: "Lord, give me the courage to change the things I can change, to accept the things I can't change, and the wisdom to know the difference."

Is this a stoic prayer or a Christian prayer? What's the difference? How is contentment different from stoicism? Is there a difference between contentment and resignation? Is there a difference between contentment and laziness? How can Christians be content without being indifferent? What's the difference between having a good work ethic and being a workaholic? Is "accepting things as they are" a Christian concept or a Greek philosophical concept? Or is there some overlap?

Discuss Gender Differences and Satisfaction

Ask, Do you think men and women tend to be discontented about different things? What are men most discontented about? What are women most discontented about? Who are most likely to verbalize their complaints—men or women? In addition to verbalizing complaints, how else do people express their discontent?

Discuss Financial Status and Contentment

Discuss the association between contentment and financial success? Do you think rich people are more content than poor people? (This raises an additional question: How do you define "rich" and "poor"?) Do you think people ought to be more content when they reach a certain point of financial security? Should they ever reach a point where they think they have enough? What is that point?

Discuss Ways to Raise Positive Children

Children often accuse their parents of nagging and putting them down by complaining about the way they dress and comb (or dye) their hair, about their untidy rooms, about their homework, and about their friends. Is this charge ever justified? How can parents encourage their children to move in the right direction without seeming to be negative and nagging?

Study Contentment and the Media

To demonstrate how the media cultivates our discontent, ask every class member to bring a printed ad or to record or summarize a television ad that encourages us to be unsatisfied and, of course, to find fulfillment by purchasing the advertiser's product or service. Don't forget the loan companies that encourage people to go into debt in order to buy things that will bring them happiness or to pay off the cost of previous efforts to buy happiness.

Close with a Positive Prayer

Ask group members to close with prayers that are filled with praise, appreciation, and thanksgiving—prayers that emphasize the positive side even of negative events.

A Beautiful Tongue Is a Simple Tongue

J esus identified children as role models for adults. "I tell you the truth," he said, "unless you change and become like little children, you will never enter the kingdom of heaven. Therefore, whoever humbles himself like this child is the greatest in the kingdom of heaven" (Matt. 18:3–4). Little children have not yet learned the niceties of public deception and deliberate obfuscation. They say what they think—which is sometimes humorous, sometimes painful, and sometimes both. They have the grace of simplicity.

Jesus, on the other hand, had harsh words for the religious leaders of the day who made every effort to appear more saintly, more devoted, and more godly than others. "Woe to you, Pharisees, because you love the most important seats in the synagogues and greetings in the marketplaces" (Luke 11:43). "Woe to you, teachers of the law and Pharisees, you hypocrites! You are like whitewashed tombs, which look beautiful on the outside but on the inside are full of dead men's bones and everything unclean" (Matt. 23:27).

Discuss Religious Expressions Designed to Impress

Discuss ways that people try to exhibit how religious they are, how moral they are, how generous they are, how committed they are. Can you think of modern parallels to the Pharisees praying on the street corners? What is the difference between Christian witnessing and Christian boasting? Do you think the church sometimes encourages people to emphasize the positive and discourages them from sharing their needs and weaknesses?

Discuss Reinforcement Expressions

As a group, discuss the way people reinforce their statements with expressions like, "I swear on a stack of Bibles," "Hope to die, stick a needle in my eye," and "As God is my witness." Suggest similar expressions that go beyond stating the simple truth. Discuss the pros and cons of these expressions.

Discuss Simplicity and Money

Discuss ways that people try to appear more affluent than they are. Include the things they buy and the things they say. Does the desire to appear affluent contribute to today's massive credit card debt?

Do Research on Prayer Language

Assign a group from your class to scour home, church,

and public libraries for books of prayer, both public and private (books *of* prayer, not *about* prayer). Analyze the language used in the prayers. Some may be highly traditional, with a lot of "thees," "thous," and "beseeches." Others may be very contemporary, even chummy. Still others may seem designed to impress people rather than to guide their words. How are these prayers helpful? How are they not helpful?

Talk About Christmas Letters

Each year in December Ann Landers prints a typical Christmas letter that is intended to impress friends while pretending to be nonchalant. It's hilarious. Write one as a group, mentioning such things as the two days of cloudy weather during the cruise, the scratch on the door of the new BMW, how surprised Junior was when he got all As on his report card, and how busy Hubby is after having been appointed vice president of the company.

Write Letters to Yourselves

You have now come to the end of this study. It's hoped that members of the class have done more than just study and that they have made serious commitments about the use of their tongues in everyday life. We are now suggesting an exercise designed to encourage long-range positive results.

Bring enough pens, stationery, and stamped envelopes for everyone in the class. Provide space for class members to spread out in at least a semiprivate manner, and provide hard surfaces (tables, clipboards, or books) to write on.

Write on the chalkboard the nine adjectives that

characterize a beautiful tongue as studied by this class: silent, appreciative, witnessing, clean, kind, nongossiping, truthful, positive, and simple.

Ask each class member to write a letter to himself or herself, address the envelope, and seal the envelope. After six months you, the class leader, will mail the letter to them. Assure them of absolute privacy; no one will see the letter except the author.

Referring to the nine topics on the board, suggest that class members

1. be honest in spelling out, in respect to their own tongues, the areas of strength and areas that need additional work;
2. describe any new insights gained during the course of this study;
3. commit themselves to certain goals concerning the use of their tongues.

Personal aspirations and intentions should be identified as specifically as possible.

Close with Prayer

As the class comes to a close, engage in an extended period of prayer, and invite class members to express their confessions, thanks, aspirations, and commitments in the use of the tongue.